KEY SIGNIFIER AS LITERARY DEVICE

KEY SIGNIFIER AS LITERARY DEVICE

Its Definition and Function
in Literature and Media

Heerak Christian Kim

The Edwin Mellen Press
Lewiston•Queenston•Lampeter

Library of Congress Cataloging-in-Publication Data

Kim, Heerak Christian
    Key signifier as literary device : its definition and function in literature and media / Heerak Christian Kim.
        p. cm.
    Includes bibliographical references and index.
    ISBN-13: 978-0-7734-5524-5
    ISBN-10: 0-7734-5524-8
    I. Title.

hors série.

A CIP catalog record for this book is available from the British Library.

The Edwin Mellen Press
Box 450
Lewiston, New York
USA 14092-0450

The Edwin Mellen Press
Box 67
Queenston, Ontario
CANADA L0S 1L0

The Edwin Mellen Press, Ltd.
Lampeter, Ceredigion, Wales
UNITED KINGDOM SA48 8LT

Printed in the United States of America

Dedicated to my mother and father

For their constant support and encouragement

Table of Contents

Preface

Professor Heerak Christian Kim is perhaps the most prolific scholar in the world today. Professor Kim has delivered academic papers at many important international academic conferences around the world, including the American Academy of Religion conference, American Schools of Oriental Research conference, American Oriental Society conference, Society of Biblical Literature Annual Meeting, British New Testament Conference, the Continental Conference of Australia and New Zealand in Religious Studies (ANZATS). Professor Kim has published many important academic books, particularly in the area of Jewish studies and the history of Christianity, such as *Jewish Law and Identity: Academic Essays*. Professor Kim never fails to wow in his creativity, erudition, and encyclopaedic knowledge of his field.

This book is a testimony to the genius of Professor Kim. This book is a tribute to the surprising potential of creative research that can be conducted by a human being. The knowledge contained in these pages is mind boggling. Each chapter represents ground breaking analysis of the subject being discussed. Chapter 1 expands on the definition of the Key Signifier, a literary term that was created by Professor Kim and coined as a literary term. The strength of this literary term is in that it allows the scholar and the general reader to understand the intentionality of the literary work. In this regard, Professor Kim has succeeded in solving the problem that has plagued literary critics and scholars of literature, both ancient and modern, for a long time. It is one thing to understand and describe intertextuality or dependence of a work, but how can we understand intentionality? Furthermore, this chapter explains how the Key Signifier as a literary phenomenon can open a door to a world of signified meaning and historical experience via a word or a phrase.

The following chapters provide examples from a myriad of literatures and other types of works of art, such as movies. Chapter 2 describes Key Signifiers in the Bible. Professor Kim shines in this examination, especially as he describes how the Key Signifier of the Purim and the Esther Tradition in the Old Testament was utilized in the New Testament. This chapter alone marks this book as an academic work of lasting merit. He opens the door to New Testament research. And having studied theology in Toronto and Yale before pursuing my study of Korean history at Harvard, I can honestly say that his research in this area opens up a world of research possibilities for New Testament scholars. I am convinced that this chapter alone will spur new monographs of academic distinction in the area of New Testament research.

Chapter 3 discusses the Key Signifier in the Pseudepigrapha. He has delivered many academic papers in this area around the world and is respected by Pseudepigrapha experts from Israel to the USA to Singapore in Asia. Quite a number of Korean scholars are building their research on his work on the Pseudepigrapha. His discussion of the Psalms of Solomon and its use of Old Testament Key Signifier from the Patriarchal Narratives of Abraham is insightful and expertly describes how the Key Signifier functioned in ancient literature. The methodology employed in the examination of this ancient Jewish work can be applied to the study of other ancient literatures, such as works by Roman writers from the age of Emperor Augustus, building on ancient Greek literature.

Chapter 4 makes the Key Signifier relevant for modern literature. Professor Kim is recognized as an emerging scholar in African-American theology as he has published in this field and is continuing to deliver academic papers in this academic discipline at internationally recognized conferences. As I understand, he is working on a definitive work on African-American theology based on Toni Morrison's books to be published in a few years' time. This chapter clearly shows why Professor Kim has gained a following among experts of African-American theology in the United States. His examination of *Beloved* is not only interesting and creative but provides a blue print for how the Key Signifier can be studied in modern literature.

Chapter 5 provides an excellent example of how a global study of literature can be accomplished. The Key Signifier can work across cultures and languages and national barriers. In an increasingly globalizing world and in the context of academia that seeks interdisciplinary studies on a global level, this chapter provides answers in terms of methodology to global academic inquiry. "Mao Zedong" by Ai Qing is a very famous poem in China. This monograph will introduce Ai Qing to many western literary experts who have yet to discover the literary world of Asia. Certainly, not only experts of literature in China, but all over Asia, including Korea, can utilize the methodology introduced in this book. I foresee great many books emerging from Korea, certainly, utilizing this book and the methodology to study the Key Signifier in Korean literature in the context of Korean history.

Chapter 6 discusses the function of the Key Signifier in media. Often, works examining literary devices fail to adequately examine literary device as applied in every day life. This chapter avoids that pitfall. This chapter provides a wealth of research potential in the field of Communications as well as academic study of film and media production. I particularly commend Professor Kim for examining *Hum Dil De Chuke Sanam*, a famous Bollywood film from India. This provides an opportunity for western film makers to step outside of their comfort zone of American films and understand the functioning of the Key Signifier in movies. Besides providing a technical lesson for western film makers in the use of the Key Signifier in film, this chapter opens up the world of Asian cinema to western audiences. Professor Kim's sensitivity to global literature and art must be applauded.   There is no doubt that each chapter will spur new academic monographs and new Ph.D. theses around the world.

I have no doubt that this book will remain in the collective consciousness of academics around the world across disciplines and in different departments. This is a ground breaking work not only in the area of literary criticism but also in the areas of history, sociology, anthropology, and comparative religious studies.

Professor Kim has taught undergraduates at Brown University and the University of California, Los Angeles, and graduate students in India, Russia, Indonesia, and the Philippines.   This book brings sensitivity to the needs of students.   This book contains cutting edge academic propositions but is readily readable by university students and the educated public.   Thus, this book has a staying power that is missing from many academic monographs that are accessible only to a handful of scholars in their field.   I have no doubt that this book will impact not only the academic world but the general intellectual world at large.   Furthermore, I can see artists, writers, poets, and film-makers impacted by this book with the result that their works of art will show a clear fingerprint of Professor Heerak Christian Kim's creative erudition.

Professor Jai Keun Choi
Professor of Korean History
Yonsei University
Seoul, South Korea

Acknowledgement

I would like to thank many scholars for their direct and personal contribution to my growth as a scholar. In particular, I would like to thank academics at the Hebrew University of Jerusalem in Israel, where I spent over three years of academic research on the professional level as a Visiting Research Scholar (1993-94), a Raoul Wallenberg Scholar (1995-96), and a Lady Davis Fellow (1996-97). I have conversed with and learned from so many Israeli scholars during that time that I cannot mention every person by name. However, I would like to mention specifically Israeli scholars who have made the greatest impact on my intellectual development: Professor Avi Hurvitz (Department of Hebrew and Aramaic), Professor Michael Stone (Department of Comparative Religion), and Professor Daniel Schwartz (Department of Jewish History). I would also so like to thank Professor Eileen Schuller of McMaster University in Canada for allowing me to read her unpublished academic papers on the Thanksgiving Psalms (1QH and 4QH) when she was a visiting scholar in Israel at the neighboring W. F. Albright Institute of Archaelogical Research in Jerusalem. While I was a Lady Davis Fellow, Allen Kerkeslager was a Fulbright Scholar in Jerusalem, completing his Ph.D. for the University of Pennsylvania under Professor Robert Kraft, researching the Egyptian Jewish community. We have shared many interesting conversations both at the Hebrew University of Jerusalem and at the same church we attended, King of Kings, an Assemblies of God charismatic church made up of Christians from Israeli, Palestinian, and foreign backgrounds. Now, Allen is a tenured professor at St. Joseph's University in Philadelphia.

I would also like to thank academics in the Diaspora who have impacted my development as a scholar. In particular, I would like to recognize Professor Marinus de Jonge of Leiden University in Holland and Professor Gerd Theissen of Heidelberg University. Professor Gerd Theissen actually took me into his home for a couple of weeks when I was apartment searching in Heidelberg for my research stay in Heidelberg. I thank him and Mrs. Theissen for their kindness, generosity, and support. Also, I would like to thank Professor William Horbury, who shared many wonderful conversations on Judaism with me. As the Professor of Hebrew, Jewish, and Early Christian Studies at the University of Cambridge for many years, he has guided Jewish Studies in Great Britain. He is arguably the most important expert in ancient Judaism today in Great Britain. I would like to thank him for his kind acceptance of my differing views and for his encouragement. His friendship and support means a lot to me.

Introduction

When we read a poem, we are deeply impacted by the imagery and the language employed by the poem, especially if the poet is very good. Without any knowledge of literary criticism and literary techniques, we can understand and appreciate the poem on emotive and cognitive levels. And we are moved by the poem. And sometimes, the poem will encourage us to do something – like send a flower to the one who is loved. It is possible that the poem can make us sad or happy. The poem can make us mad or furious. We do not need any knowledge of academic study of poems to understand, appreciate, and be affected by a poem.

Poetry has moved every known society for this simple reason. It can be appreciated by everyone on a base level. Whether listened to or read, a poem can have a deep impact on the educated as well as the uneducated. Poetry is often the common property of the greatest percentage of the population. The fact that poems are short often makes them accessible to a greater population. Whereas a novel requires patience and regular reading, a poem gives instant satisfaction. One can read a poem in a few minutes, and many poems fit into a single page. Memory work is not required as it would be with a novel or even a short story. It may be short and it may be read in an hour or two, but a short story has characters and plot and intrigue which require intellectual work and memory. With a poem, one can just read it and be quickly impacted by it and then put it down. The short length and easy accessibility of poetry is what gives it such deep power over other forms of literary expression.

Of course, there are long poems. Some poems are meant to be read as an epic, such as *The Odyssey* and *The Iliad* by Homer. And these epic poems will indicate that large works of poetry can be even more complex than novels and short stories. However, these are exceptions that prove the rule. Poetry tends to be short and easily accessible, not requiring much education to understand.

Although poetry seems disarmingly simplistic on many levels, to assume it to be devoid of complexity is to ignore its true identity. What is, in fact, beautiful about poetry is that any reader or listener can appreciate the aesthetics of poems without fully understanding their complexity. In a way, the complexity of the poem functions in the background and often on a subconscious level.

As tempting as it is to leave complexity aside, it would not be fair to the identity of poetry to ignore its complex, yet beautiful, depth. And for academics and intellectuals, it becomes a matter of integrity to explore the complexity beyond the surface reading (*peshat* in Hebrew) of the text.

There are many books written on poetic devices and literary techniques used in poetry. Terms such as alliteration, simile, metaphor quickly come to mind for anyone who has engaged in an academic study of poetry or read an intellectual book on the subject.

In this book, I will discuss some of these poetic techniques. But I will discuss them in relation to the literary technique that I am introducing in the book – namely, the key signifier. "Key signifier" is obviously comprised of two words, "key" and "signifier." Of course, we have all heard of these words before. And some of us may have even used the term "key signifier" before or have read the term being used. But it has never been used in an official way. What I mean by that is that the term "key signifier" has not been used as a defined, literary device term, before. This is due to the simple reason that I have coined the term. I have defined the term in the context of academic conferences and academic publications as a specific term to indicate a literary device used in the writing of poetry or other works of literature. As far as I am aware, there is no publication on the literary device of the "key signifier" except mine – certainly, not in the way I have defined it. Perhaps in the future, there will be academic works as well as literary pieces building on my foundational research work on the topic.

In fact, this book represents a first holistic presentation of the nature and function of the key signifier. Once you have read the book, you will see the importance of the literary device of the key signifier and the significance of understanding its nature and usage. After reading this book, your eyes will be opened and you will be able to detect key signifiers in poetry and other types of writing and speech.

This is not so dissimilar to being enlightened to the function of the metaphor. It is possible to appreciate metaphor even before studying it and understanding its nature and function. But after studying the characteristics of the metaphor, it opens your eyes. You begin to see metaphors and identify them as such in light of your understanding of the nature and function of metaphors.

In the similar way, you will come to understand and appreciate the nature and function of the key signifier after reading this book. What is a key signifier? I will state the definition I presented to the scholars in the Apocrypha and Pseudepigrapha Section of the 2005 International Meeting of the Society of Biblical Literature in Singapore (June 26 – July 1, 2005). "A key signifier is defined as a term or phrase that triggers a collective memory or a community value that is over-arching and all-encompassing. A key signifier functions aggressively in the literary context to spur audience to action."[1]

Of course, this definition of the key signifier was not developed in 2005 but was "in the making" for many years. I coined the term in my study of the Psalms of Solomon, a poetry work from a couple of hundred years before Jesus Christ. The Psalms of Solomon is a work of poetry by Jews in the Late Second Temple period. As the work of poetry was passed down, there were redactions

---

[1] Heerak Christian Kim, "The Key Signifier of 'Forever' in Psalms of Solomon 11," *Jewish Law and Identity: Academic Essays* (Cheltenham: The Hermit Kingdom Press, 2005), p. 212.

and modifications. As you can imagine, the Psalms of Solomon is a complex piece of poetic work in the form that we have it, today.

For the purposes of this book, which is to explain the nature and function of the literary device of the key signifier, it is not necessary to dive into the redaction history of the Psalms of Solomon. In this book, we will examine the Psalms of Solomon only insofar as it can shed light on the nature and function of the literary device of the key signifier.

Let us examine the definition of key signifier further. We notice that there are two components to the key signifier. First, there is the reference to the past (or present). This idea is encompassed in the two phrases, "collective memory" and "community value." There cannot be collective memory unless there was some kind of collective experience in the past that captured the imagination of the whole population. The experience can be a lived experience, such as experiencing a national independence. July 4th as the Independence Day is in the collective memory of the American people because it is an experience that was lived through by all Americans at the time. The collective memory of fighting together, soldiers dying, and gaining national independence came to be ingrained in the national psyche – of the descendants of those who fought in the Revolutionary War and those who came to call themselves, "American."

But collective memory does not have to be a lived experience as such. It is possible to develop collective memory based on a type of imagined experience that captures the imagination of a people. A good example of this would be *The Da Vinci Code* by Dan Brown. This novel took the American population by surprise and captured the interests of many Americans. There were Americans who loved the book. There were Americans who hated the book. But it is undeniable that the book was a phenomenon which engraved itself in the collective memory of the American people.

One can see that the collective memory involved with *The Da Vinci Code* is completely different from the collective memory of the Revolutionary War.

The Revolutionary War was a lived experience that became a part of the collective memory. In contrast, *The Da Vinci Code* was a book that impacted the collective consciousness of the American people, although there was no experience as such tied to the book. Any experience would only have been on a cognitive level. Thus, we can call this "an imagined experience."

Despite the fact that *The Da Vinci Code* was an imagined experience, and not a lived experience, its impact on the collective memory of the American people is profound. Perhaps, in the context of 21st century America, it is more profound and deep than the collective memory of the Revolutionary War. Thus, we recognize that imagined experiences can potentially have a greater impact on collective memory than a lived experience.

It is important to emphasize that whether collective memory is based on lived experience, such as the American Revolution, or on imagined experience, such as *The Da Vinci Code*, the collective memory is based on something from the past or the present that captures the collective consciousness of a people. In other words, there is something that can trigger the collective memory – there is a strong referent from the past or present.

In the two part definition of the key signifier, the first part of the definition, as we recall, is: "A key signifier is defined as a term or phrase that triggers a collective memory or a community value that is over-arching and all-encompassing." We have discussed what "collective memory" is and how it relates to a past or present referent. We will discuss the other element, namely "community value" that also has an important function to trigger the collective consciousness attached to the past (or the present).

What is a community value? On a simplistic level, "collective memory" and "community value" can be described as interchangeable. The Revolutionary War is a collective memory that relates to the American community value of national independence and the right of a people to rule themselves. One can argue that the two elements are inseparable. However, even this example shows that "collective memory" is not necessarily interchangeable with "community value." It is possible to treasure the Revolutionary War as a community without necessarily valuing the right of a people to govern themselves. For instance, not all who value the Revolutionary War agree that the Palestinians should have a right to govern themselves or that Scotland has the right to collect its own taxes and declare independence from England. "Collective memory" and "community value" are not really interchangeable.

Whereas collective memory is based on a shared lived experience or an imagined experience, a community value is related to a belief system. There may be a belief system attached to the Revolutionary War, but it is difficult to identify which belief system this is. In the like manner, there may be a belief system attached to *The Da Vinci Code*, but again it is difficult to identify what belief system this is. Because collective memory is based on experience, either lived or imagined, belief system can be peripheral to that experience and to the collective memory. On the other hand, community value is necessarily tied to a belief system that can be described and systematized.

For example, we can say that a community value for Americans is democracy. Democracy is a belief system that can be described and systematized. When we talk about democracy, we often associate values of freedom, liberty, and individual rights. Community value is a belief system that the community agrees is important, on an active level or a passive level.

But it is important to recognize the difficulties involved when we try to find agreement on finer details of a mentioned community value. Let us examine "democracy" for instance. Is democracy a rule by the majority? Or is democracy a protection of all individual rights, even including the "aberrant minority member"? These two definitions of democracy can be mutually exclusive. In other words, the two definitions are not compatible with each other. For instance, if democracy is a rule by the majority, then the policies of "democracy" must privilege the majority opinion, first and foremost, and, if need be, subjugate the opinions of the minority. But if democracy is a protection of all individual rights, even including the "aberrant minority member", the definition can be stretched to defend a small group of people who may even pose a threat to the majority. Protecting the interests of a small group of minority can, in fact, be detrimental to the interests of the majority of the population. It is interesting to note that, in fact, this is the current debate regarding democracy that is raging in American democracy. Currently, the latter definition is operating as the consensus, but that does not mean that the latter definition is accepted by the majority of Americans or even by many Americans (in relative terms).

The same can be said for freedom, liberty, and individual rights. What do we mean by these things? In terms of freedom, it will be hard to find an American going on record to state that freedom implies the freedom to rape a 11 year old girl. By liberty, most will not say that it refers to the liberty to burn down a church. By individual rights, hardly anyone will go on record to say that it refers to the individual rights to invade any property at will any time of the day. Although many will be agreed one what freedom, liberty, and individual rights may not refer to, it is more difficult to find out what they do refer to.

What then is "communal value"? A communal value can be substantiated and systematized to an extent. But a true communal value is what German scholars have called *Zeitgeist* or "the spirit of the age." It is hard to quantify in every detail. In the American context, it is possible to say that Christianity is a communal value. We can make this statement based on the fact that over 90 percent of Americans call themselves Christians of some sort. Since Christianity is a system that is written about, it is possible to describe what the communal value of Christianity is in generic terms. On a functional level, such a description can be helpful to understand the communal value of a people. Besides descriptive texts on Christianity, there are also core religious texts (or foundational texts) that are integrally a part of the religion. Examining these things helps us get closer to what the communal value is. But of course, from time to time, communal values based on religious texts change. That is why the best way to describe communal value is in terms of *Zeitgeist* It is not always easy to identify *Zeitgeist* and that is why most of the quantitative studies on communal values are based on religious texts.

Certainly, we can state that for something to be described as a community value, there must be some kind of social contract that is arrived at invisibly or unconsciously, in the least. In this regard, collective memory and community value share similarities; there has to be a collective consent to the communal worth of a "memory" or "value."

What a key signifier does is to trigger these systems – "a collective memory" or "a communal value" (and potentially, these elements functioning together). Thus, we have discussed the first part of the two-part definition for the key signifier. "A key signifier is defined as a term or phrase that triggers a collective memory or a community value that is over-arching and all-encompassing."

What about the second part of the two-part definition? If we recall, the second part of the definition for the key signifier is: "A key signifier functions aggressively in the literary context to spur audience to action." The second part of the definition refers to the functional aspect of the key signifier as a literary device. Not only does the key signifier recall a collective memory or a communal value, it prompts the listener or reader to act based on that recall.

In fact, it is the functional aspect of the key signifier that sets it apart from other literary devices described that may resemble a part of the nature of the key signifier. For instance, "echo" is a term used to describe the literary device of repeating something from before. So, an idea from the past can be echoed. Or collective memory can be solicited via an echo. Maybe an echo will recall a communal value. However similar "echo" as a literary device may be to the key signifier, it is completely different in its fundamental nature. There is no action solicited by the echo as a part of its very nature. In contrast, the key signifier is not a key signifier if it does not spur the listener or reader to action. It is the very fact of action-producing, functional aspect of the word or phrase that defines it as a key signifier.

In other words, a word or phrase cannot be a key signifier if it only recalls a collective memory or a community value. In such a case, a better term to use to describe what is going is to use the word "echo" to describe things. As we have shown, the key signifier has a two-part definition. If one of the two parts is missing, then the word or phrase cannot be a key signifier.

In the like manner, a word or phrase that prompts the reader or the listener to action but does not fulfil the first part of the definition of the key signifier in recalling the collective memory or the community value cannot be a key signifier. For a word or phrase to be a key signifier, it has to satisfy the requirements of both parts of the definition of key signifier outlined above.

Let us dive a little bit more into the second part of the two-part definition: "A key signifier functions aggressively in the literary context to spur audience to action." In order to understand what this means, it may be good to go to an example that can help explain the function of the key signifier. If a person says, "fire!" in a crowded building, what is he doing? He is soliciting an action from the listeners. He is not saying, "fire!" in order to have people merely look at him. Saying "fire" in a crowded building is intentionally meant to produce a reaction. In a way, it is possible to say that the word "fire" in the very context of a crowded building has a trigger mechanism built into it.

What is the word "fire" supposed to do? It is meant to spur listeners to action, and the action is to find the fire escape and find a way to leave the building. Why does the word "fire" produce this kind of an effect? Because people associate the word "fire" with a reality attached to that word – namely, fire that can kill them. Thus, one does not have to say, "run!" or "jump!" for people to follow such a course of action. All one has to say is, "fire!"

If we understand the trigger mechanism of saying "fire" in a crowded building, then we can better understand the trigger mechanism of the key signifier. In the same way that saying "fire" produces the result of people running toward the fire exit to leave the building and jumping off the windows of the building to safety, a key signifier produces a concrete action without spelling out what that concrete action should be. To an extent, we can say that "fire" in the context of saying it in a crowded building has attributes that it shares with the literary device of the key signifier. "Fire!" recalls a collective memory of what fire does and can do to their lives and it compels the audience to act based on that collective memory.

"Fire" in this context illustrates another aspect of the key signifier. There are only several set of actions (such as running toward the fire exit or jumping out of the window) that a key signifier is intended to produce. Often, the key signifier aims at producing a singular action and not multiple (and certainly not contradictory) set of actions. To use the example of "fire" further, we can say that if someone says "fire!" in a crowded building, you would not expect someone to start lighting a cigarette. You would not expect people to start a conversation with the person next to them about work. You would not have people wanting to go to bathroom to relieve themselves. Saying "fire" in a crowded building is meant to produce one set of actions – namely, to have people leave the building.

That is not to say that there won't be some people who won't follow the set of actions meant to be spurred by saying "fire!" in a crowded building. Someone may say, "Gosh, that really makes me want to go to the bathroom." He may proceed thereafter to go to the bathroom. But this is not an expected behavior or an intended one. In fact, most people would find such an action odd or strange. Some may think that he is crazy. It is easy to see why this example serves as an exception that proves the rule.

This is the case with the key signifier. The key signifier is intended to produce a set of actions that are unified in terms of content and purpose. There may be people who digress from the intended purpose of the key signifier, but that represents an aberration and not the norm. The example of "fire" is particularly helpful for explaining the key signifier because by nature, the key signifier does not spell out or explain the action sought after.

Saying "fire" in a crowded place is saying something else in a sense. It is meant to produce action that has really nothing to do with the word "fire" per se. Running for an exit does not have any semantic sharing of connotative congruence with the word "fire" intrinsically. Jumping off the window has no real association with the word "fire" in terms of word root or etymology or meaning. The reason that the association exists between the word "fire" and the intended action solicited by the word is because of collective memory and community value that are shared.

This is precisely what the key signifier is. The key signifier in and of itself has no visible or audible association with the action that it is soliciting. The only way one can understand the association is through the lens of a collective memory and a community value. But like "fire," the key signifier in a poem or in speech is meant to solicit a concrete action that is not spelled out in any way. It is because of collective memory or community value, that listeners or readers instinctively understand the action sought. And just like "fire," the key signifier will produce action.

In this regard, a word or phrase cannot be a key signifier if it does not produce an action. It is also important to reiterate that a word or phrase cannot be a key signifier if it indicates in any way the action sought. By definition, the key signifier recalls a collective memory or a community value to trigger an action. And the resultant action is a proof of the key signifier. Just like saying "fire" will produce results, the key signifier will necessarily produce results.

The job of the literary critic and scholar investigating key signifiers in a poem or in a spoken text is to analyze which collective memory or community value those key signifiers recall and to assess what kind of action the key signifiers are intended to produce and actually produce. In a sense, therefore, a literary critic examining key signifiers cannot be purely literary critics. There is a historical dimension that cannot be ignored. There is a cause and an effect. Thus, the key signifier must bring in historical criticism (or historiography) to explain the nature and function of an identified key signifier.

When we sit down to think about the implication of the intellectual enterprise involved in identifying the nature and function of key signifiers in any text, we can see why the key signifier as a literary device is so significant. Correctly identifying a key signifier opens the door to that community's value system. It is a testimony to the fact that the identifier of the key signifier actually understands not only the literary material in front of him but also the signifying world behind the text. Not only that, he actually understand the current community to which the text is addressed so much that he can correctly identify the intended affect.

Correctly identifying the nature and function of a key signifier in a particular text is, therefore, a gargantuan task. It requires historical and sociological knowledge not typically expected of a literary critic. Identifying "simile" and "metaphor" does not require the knowledge of a collective memory or a community value per se. All that the literary critic has to do is to understand the denotation of the word as such. Any knowledge beyond that is a cherry on the top of an ice cream Sunday.

Identifying key signifiers in a text is a difficult enterprise, and it requires multi-disciplinary approach to a text. In a way, the key signifier represents what is possible in a humanistic study that combines the contribution of various academic fields and departments. This book will help explain the nature and function of the key signifier as a literary device. And we will also examine some concrete examples that will help illuminate the literary device in actual operation.

Chapter 1

The Nature of the Key Signifier

In this chapter, we will build on the definition of the key signifier provided in the introduction. If we recall, "A key signifier is defined as a term or phrase that triggers a collective memory or a community value that is over-arching and all-encompassing. A key signifier functions aggressively in the literary context to spur audience to action." Now that we understand basically what a key signifier is, we will discuss in greater depth the nature and content of the key signifier. In other words, we will examine the extent of the denotation and the connotation of the key signifier.

There are a few fundamental questions related to the nature of the key signifier, and these questions relate to the nature of collective memory and community value, the nature of the trigger mechanism, and the nature of the impact on the audience – either listeners or readers. Let us approach this systematically from the beginning of the list to the end of the list.

Firstly, what is the nature of "collective memory" and "community value"? We have touched on this question somewhat in the introduction in the process of explaining the definition for the key signifier. Here, we will expand on our explanation and study the wider implications of the nature of "collective memory" and "community value." To a certain extent, collective memory and community value overlap. However, as indicated in the introduction, it is important to recognize that they are not the same. In fact, they can be mutually exclusive.

Since they are distinctively different identities, we will discuss them separately. First, we will begin our discussion of collective memory.

Collective memory is a funny thing, from one vantage point. I use the word "funny" because it is really quite difficult to quantify. What impacts collective memory? It is really hard to predict what will make an impact. Often, we know something to be in the collective memory because of the effect or the result. Something becomes a part of the collective memory, and we know them to be a part of the collective memory because there is a ubiquitous use of it.

A good example of this is found in the term "the 1.5 generation." This is a term in the collective memory of all Korean-Americans who consider themselves Korean-Americans. No one really knows who started the phrase. There is not a single monograph explaining its conception, history, definition, and nature. There are a few articles, most notably by Professor Won Moo Hurh. But even Korean-American scholars use the term 1.5 without must attention to defining it. It is assumed that the readers and listeners know the definition.

And it is true. Among the Korean-Americans, everyone knows the definition – it is a part of the Korean-American collective memory. Everyone instinctively knows what it is because the term is ubiquitous and used by everyone. Those outside of the Korean-American community struggle to understand what a 1.5 generation is. Professor Won Moo Hurh defines the 1.5 generation Korean-American in this way:

> At this point of discussion, however, the 1.5 generation can ideally-typically be defined as bilingual and bicultural Korean-American who immigrated to the United States in early or middle adolescence (generally between the ages of 11 and 16). Simply put, the adolescent immigration, bilingualism, and biculturalism constitute a unique sociocultural and existential context of Korean-American whose life course appears to be quite different from that of the first and second generation immigrants.[2]

---

[2] Won Moo Hurh, "The 1.5 Generation: A Cornerstone of the Korean-American Ethnic Community," *The Emerging Generation of Korean-Americans*, eds. Ho-Youn Kwon and Shin Kim (Seoul: Kyung Hee University Press, 1993, pp. 47-79), p. 50.

By first generation immigrants, Professor Hurh is referring to Korean adult immigrants from Korea. In relation to the 1.5, the first generation Korean immigrants tend to be their parents. Thus, when a young married couple in their thirties immigrated to the United States, they may have had young children with them, who would be considered 1.5.

Second generation Korean immigrants refer to Koreans who are born in America but who have parents who were born in Korea (or other countries besides the USA). There may be some confusion among non-Koreans regarding the reality of what Korean-Americans refer to as 2nd generation. A question may be raised: Isn't it possible for a young couple in their twenties to immigrate to the United States and have all their children in the USA? It is possible and they would be all referred to as 2nd generation. A question may be pursued further. What if 1.5 have children who are born in the USA, what are they? They are not 2.5. There is no such term in the Korean-American community. The decimal system only applies between the 1st generation and 2nd generation Koreans.

In this system developed and entrenched in the collective memory of the Korean-American population, everyone instinctively knows that children born in America to 1.5 are 2nd generation. This may seem contradictory or confusing to non-Korean-Americans. It is understandable because they are outsiders. They are not a part of the collective memory of the Korean-American population. The collective memory in regards to the term "1.5 generation" only applies to Korean-Americans.

1.5 generation is not a term that is available to any other Asian-American communities, either. In this regard, the term is specifically Korean-American and exclusively so. Professor Won Moo Hurh writes about this reality:

> The tem was coined in the Korean community around 1980. Although the Japanese term for first-, second-, and third-generation immigrants – *issei*, *nisei*, and *sansei* – are found in *Webster's*

16

16

> *Dictionary*, a term such as '1.5 generation' has not been used with
> reference to other immigrant groups.[3]

In this sense, the term "1.5 generation" is an exclusive part of the collective memory of Korean-Americans.

The fact that "1.5 generation" came out of nowhere and was "coined" communally without any one individual defining it or any book explaining it explains the spontaneous nature of this collective memory. We do not really know the causes or the reasons for the generation of this term. We do not even know the precise cause-and-effect that made this term stick in the Korean-American community. We are not sure how individual Korean-Americans started to use this term. We know that sometime in the 1980s, this term was being used as ubiquitously in the Korean-American community like the term "USA" or "Korea". Everyone in the Korean-American community understood what 1.5 meant. In a sense, we know that 1.5 is a part of the Korean collective memory because of the result that it is being used ubiquitously.

The process can be described as a kind of popular phenomenon. I think that word "funny" can explain the whole situation. Anyone outside of the Korean-American community would find the term confusing and strange – in other words, "funny." But no Korean-American is confused by the term or think of the term as strange. 1.5 is solidly entrenched in the collective memory of the Korean-American community.

Because 1.5 is a part of the collective memory of the Korean-American community, it is easy to see how it can be used potentially as a key signifier. All a Korean-American has to do is to use the term "1.5" and it triggers the collective memory to all the ideas and experiences attached to the 1.5 generation in the historical experience of Korean-Americans. The limitation of this book does not allow me to go into an indepth discussion of the Korean-American immigration experiences and other associative experiences, literature, and ideas linked to the

---

[3] Won Moo Hurh, *The Korean Americans* (Westport: Greenwood Press, 1998), p. 164.

1.5 generation. However, for the purposes of this book, being able to understand the import of "1.5 generation" for the Korean-American collective memory suffices. We understand "1.5 generation" to be an integral part of the Korean-American collective memory because of the result that it is used ubiquitously as an understood terminology in the Korean-American context.

The example of the collective memory of Korean-Americans helps us understand what collective memory is. It is in the consciousness of the members of a community who share that collective memory. Collective memory can be formed spontaneously, gradually, under detection, and even intentionally.

A communal value can often be initiated and formed in the same manner as a collective memory. Like collective memory, communal value can be formed spontaneously and without anyone dictating the nature or the definition of that value. Something becomes a communal value and we know this to be the case based on result. If members of the community agree that something is a communal value – instinctively – then it is a communal value. We do not need to understand the historical development of that value or the cause-and-effect of that value to understand that something is a community value. We see it through the result on the community and the value held by the members of the community. In this manner, a communal value is very similar to collective memory.

It is important to note that community value can be prescriptive and does not necessarily have to be spontaneous or unconsciously generated. This is the case with collective memory as well. We will discuss how a communal value can be prescriptive. The best example in the American context is alcohol and Fundamentalist Christianity. America is the exporter of Fundamentalist Christianity. Fundamentalist Christianity started in America in the early 1900s, and missionaries have been spreading its teachings for decades.

Fundamentalist Christian missionaries have been quite effective, so there are Fundamentalist Christians all over the world, in every country where you will find Christianity. In fact, Fundamentalist Christianity has taken particularly strong hold in Asia and Africa. Some claim that they are now the most vocal proponents of Fundamentalist Christianity. This does not mean that Fundamentalist Christianity is dead in America. In fact, the majority of church-going Christians in America today subscribe to some element – if not all – of historic Fundamentalist Christianity. And this is the case regardless of denomination. Thus, you will find President George W. Bush, who is a mainline United Methodist, who subscribes to many of the values of Fundamentalist Christianity. There are functionally "Fundamentalist Christians" in every Christian denomination in the USA. Fundamentalist Christianity had a profound impact on America.

It is no accident that most associate prohibition to alcohol with Fundamentalist Christianity. Fundamentalist Christianity and its strength contributed to Prohibition Laws in the United States during the early half of the twentieth century. Still, prohibition to alcohol is one of the hallmarks of Fundamentalist Christianity. Many Christian colleges will require that students, staff, and professors sign a personal statement not to drink alcohol. Many of these Christian colleges deemed the very act of drinking alcohol as sin. It is a part of their collective memory and an important part of it.

Obviously, Prohibition Laws were prescriptive in nature. There were laws passed to prohibit the drinking of alcohol. The way that the United States government enforced this law was to crack down on sellers of alcohol, primarily, although those who bought alcohol and consumed them were arrested as well.

In the same way, making students, staff, and professors sign a statement that they will not drink alcohol is a prescriptive way of maintaining a community value. Anyone who enters the Christian college is expected to subscribe to the community value. Failure to heed the community value will result in expulsion or being fired. The point is that the community value is so important that it must be taught and the value maintained through active action and legislation. In

Christian communities, the language of holiness is employed to describe the purpose of the action.

Whatever the purpose may be, it is important to note that not drinking alcohol is a community value for Fundamentalist Christianity. When a Christian church or a Christian college no longer requires abstention from alcohol, it is no longer considered a Fundamentalist Christian church or school. Prohibition of alcohol is integral to the nature of Fundamentalist Christianity. Thus, to remain a Fundamentalist Christian individually or be a part of Fundamentalist Christianity, one must abstain from alcohol. It is an essential community value.

One can see how alcohol can function as a key signifier for Fundamentalist Christians and Fundamental Christian groups. The use of terms such as "wine" or "champagne" will trigger a community value (against it and those who encourage it) in Fundamentalist Christian camps. Thus, alcohol and terms associated with it can potentially function as important key signifiers for Fundamentalist Christian communities. This is possible only because prohibition to alcohol is a value in Fundamentalist Christianity.

Having identified prohibition to alcohol as a community value of Fundamentalist Christianity, we can ask the relevant question. Can we talk of it as a collective memory? Prohibition of alcohol is more appropriately described in terms of value. Whereas "1.5 generation" does not have any prohibition or requirement attached to it, so we can use the more neutral term, "memory," prohibition to alcohol does.

Although both collective memory and communal value can be formed either spontaneously or consciously, there is a fundamental difference. The difference relates to the neutrality of the element that the community holds in perpetual usage. The term "1.5 generation" does not have any requirement attached to it, whereas prohibition to alcohol does. Thus, on a simplistic level, we can distinguish between collective memory and community value in terms of requirements for the members of the community.

But in the larger context of the key signifier, both collective memory and community value function in the same way. A key signifier triggers a collective memory or a community value. In other words, the key signifier opens the semantic and experiential world of the community.

Having discussed the nature of collective memory and community value, we can now discuss the nature of the triggering mechanism attached to the literary device of the key signifier. A key signifier is a word or phrase that triggers collective memory and community value. But a word or phrase would not be a key signifier if it does not produce concrete action. Merely recalling the semantic field and experience of the past or present does not qualify a word or phrase as a key signifier.

In a sense, therefore, we can speak of double edged or dual-layered trigger function of key signifiers. A key signifier triggers collective memory and community value on the one hand, and it also triggers an action as the direct result of the first triggering. It is a very complex trigger mechanism, but one that can be analyzed and understood.

In the introduction, we have discussed crying "fire" in a crowded building. It triggers the collective memory and produces an action. People will run toward exits or jump out of the window of the building to safety. The word "fire" functions like a key signifier because it triggers the semantic and experiential field of collective memory associated with saying "fire" in a crowded building. There are actions that are expected in the very word in this context. It is the associated relationship of the triggered collective memory that allows for the expectation of a certain set of behaviors and actions.

It is important to know that the set of actions expected is integrally tied to the nature of collective memory. It is from the pool of collective memory that the listeners are able to deduce, perhaps instinctively and even subconsciously, what is expected of them. In other words, it is an integral part of a collective memory.

This example from the introduction is fairly easy in terms of identifying the dual-layered trigger mechanism. But it is not so easy with most of the key signifiers. There are nuances and complexities related with key signifiers. And it is difficult for outsiders or those in the out-group to understand the precise nature or even simple meaning of the key signifiers (or potential key signifiers). This is the case with "1.5 generation." Most people would not even know what this is without an explanation. This would be true with both the educated and the uneducated who are not a part of the in-group of Korean-Americans.

Let us discuss "1.5 generation" further with an attention to its potential as a key signifier with dual layer trigger mechanism. We have discussed at length how it relates to collective memory. Thus, we know that there is the first part of the trigger mechanism. The question to ask now is: What is its second trigger? What action does "1.5 generation" prompt? This is not as easy to identify or understand. But it is crucial that we identify this second trigger. Without it, "1.5 generation" cannot be a key signifier. Only when the dual-layered trigger mechanism is working, can we call a word or phrase a key signifier.

Of course, answering the question of the second trigger function requires a good understanding of the Korean-American community and Korean-American community's collective memory and collective (sub)consciousness. In a sense, a great intimate knowledge is required to identify the second trigger than the first trigger. The first trigger is relatively easy to identify because all you have to do is find the collective memory recalled by a word or phrase. It is always more difficult to identify the cause-and-effect or a potential effect of a word or phrase. But it is certainly possible.

So, what are potential second triggers of "1.5 generation"? In other words, if "1.5 generation" is a key signifier, what does this word/phrase prompt in the way of action? I would argue that "1.5 generation" prompts the action of Korean-loyalty and anti-white stance. This may sound generic, but upon closer examination one can see that it is definitely specific in a particular context. Before examining a specific example, let us unpack this idea on a general level.

To understand why the key signifier of "1.5 generation" will prompt an anti-white stance/action and a pro-Korean stance/action, it is important to recall what 1.5 generation is. 1.5 generation is a Korean-American who left Korea at a young age and came to the United States. By definition, 1.5 generation Korean-American has spent some time in the Korean education system. She has attended elementary school, or even junior high and high school in Korea. On the other hand, 1.5 generation Korean-American must have experienced education in America as well. A person cannot be a 1.5 generation Korean if he has not spent at least some of his high school life in the United States of America.

The emphasis, of course, is on the fact that 1.5 Korean-American has experienced both the Korean cultural and educational life and the American cultural and educational life at the age of reason. Because she has experienced both cultures, she can make a conscious decision about which culture she likes better and which culture she likes less. As can be understood, there is an expectation in the Korean-American community that if one has to choose between the two cultures, one should choose the Korean culture as more favorable, at least in theory.

The expectation is clearly there for the 1.5 generation. In other words, 1.5 generation must choose the Korean culture over the American culture in terms of preference. Choosing the American culture over the Korean culture is seen as tantamount to self-hatred and representing a hatred of the Korean community. This can be understood in terms of rejection. If a Korean-American has experienced both the Korean cultural life in the Korean context and the American cultural life in the American cultural context and opts to prefer American culture, it is a rejection of Koreans. Which Korean-Americans will appreciate such a rejection?

Unlike the 1.5 generation, 2nd and 3rd generations are somewhat exempted from this requirement to actively prefer Korea over America. The idea exists in the Korean-American community that 2nd and 3rd generation Korean-Americans never knew Korea, so how could they prefer Korea over America? Interestingly enough, however, the majority of 2nd and 3rd generation Korean-Americans aggressively prefer things Korean over and against things American. Even though they do not really know what Korea is or what Korea is like, they gravitate toward Korea. This is proven in the fact that the majority of 2nd and 3rd generation Korean-Americans actively seek out Korean cultural centers, such as the Korean-American church, on their own volition.

2nd and 3rd generation Koreans also seek out Korean friends. Many 2nd and 3rd generation Korean-Americans who went to high schools where they were the only Korean in their grade start making friendships mostly with Koreans when they go to college. This is certainly true at Harvard University and Yale University as much as it is true in a community college setting. This happens regardless of whether they can speak Korean or not.

Many in the Korean-American find this an interesting phenomenon. What the 1st generation Korean-Americans do not understand, often, is that 2nd and 3rd generation Korean-Americans gravitate toward other Koreans because of discrimination they often perceive they experience as the people of color. Being fluent in the language and culture of America, they are in tune with more subtle forms of rejection, so 2nd and 3rd generation Korean-Americans often testify that they experience rejection. For many 1st generation Korean-Americans, this is difficult to understand because it is outside their experiential scope based on their lack of complete understanding of the American culture and history.

Many scholars of the Korean-American experience, in fact, posit that those Koreans with the greatest assimilation will experience the greatest potential level of alienation from mainstream America. Professor Hurh and Professor Kim write:

> Simply put, the more closely Korean immigrants identify themselves with their WASP peers, the more they will experience heightened feelings of relative deprivation, social alienation, and identity ambivalence. At this point, the degree of the immigrant's life satisfaction (psychological adaptation) and their desire for assimilation (sociocultural adaptation) may start to decline. To mitigate the problematic situation, some immigrants may shift their reference group back to their own ethnic group (Koreans)....[4]

Certainly, this is the case with the 2nd and 3rd generation Korean-Americans.

Still, it is important to note that there is not the kind of aggressive expectation for the 2nd and 3rd generations by the Korean-American community like there is for the 1.5 generation. To a large extent, the pressure is generated by the 1.5 generation for themselves. Terms like "banana" came to be applied to those Koreans who act like they are "white on the inside" while being "yellow on the outside." Banana is a derogatory term applied to those 1.5 Korean-Americans who choose American culture over Korean culture. Often, "bananas" are shunned or excluded from Korean-American communal functions and gatherings – at least, until they renounce their "banana" ways and embrace Korean culture as their primary reference point.

Thus, one can see how "1.5 generation" can come to have the key signifier function of prompting anti-white and pro-Korean stance/action. It is interesting to note in this regard that it was the 1.5 generation which fought against the glass ceiling of admissions in Ivy League universities. Every Korean society in the Ivy League has a record of such struggles. There are differences in the degree of intensity in terms of struggle but every Korean society in the Ivy League had 1.5 generation actively fighting for Korean students' rights, particularly in the 1980s and 1990s. Of course, the history of such events is still in the process of being written.

---

[4] Won Moo Hurh and Kwang Chung Kim, *Korean Immigrants in America: A Structural Analysis of Ethnic Confinement and Adhesive Adaptation* (Rutherford: Associated University Presses, 1984), p. 140.

We can see that "1.5 generation" came to be identified with the struggle of Koreans against whites to procure rights for Korean students in the American university context. It is not difficult to see why with such experiences "1.5 generation" came to function as a key signifier in the Korean-American society. We understand this on a general level, but how about in specific settings? What kind of specific examples of the working of the literary device of the key signifier can we find operating in the term, "1.5 generation"?

In order to answer this question, let us give an example of "1.5 generation" or "1.5" being used in a specific context. Let us suppose that there is a group of people having a formal dinner in a swanky event celebrating UCLA. There is a select number of alumni gathered in this "by invitation only" event. Let us suppose the honorary speaker is the Mayor of Los Angeles, and he happens to be a white American.

There is a fund-drive for scholarships, and the select alumni in attendance are expected to make big contributions. Let us suppose that the white mayor started to ignore Koreatown and Korean residents of Los Angeles in his accolades and his illustrations about the contributors to the Los Angeles community. Some Korean-Americans are upset because their community is being glossed over by the guest speaker for the event. And UCLA organizers do not seem to be making any efforts to correct the imbalance that seems to ignore the Korean-American community, when some 70% of all Korean-Americans living in the United Sates live in the greater Los Angeles region.

One of the conscientious Korean-Americans can try to register objections to what she perceives as an anti-Korean bias of UCLA. Thus, she refuses to make a contribution to the UCLA scholarship fund. But still this is on a personal level. Her not donating $100,000 which she had intended to is only a drop in the bucket for UCLA's coffers. Also, not donating alone does nothing to improve the situation of Korean-Americans at UCLA or in Los Angeles.

This bright Korean-American woman, having received one of the best educations in the United States at UCLA, decides that she wants to encourage all the Korean-Americans not to contribute any money to the intended fund for the formal dinner to send a message to the UCLA organizers. But she does not want to make herself look bad. She may be able to grab some of her closest friends and tell them directly not to contribute any donation to UCLA. But the word can go out and the Korean-Americans she talks to blame her or criticize her. How will this Korean-American woman bring about the result that Korean-Americans not contribute any money to the fund drive? Collectively, it could be a loss of a few million dollars to the fund? It can work to empower the Korean-American community in light of the circumstances.

One thing she can do is to create an alternative funding program. For instance, she can say, "Let's create a scholarship fund for Asian-Americans with the requirement that only ethnic Asian-Americans can receive this scholarship." This is one way to send a message to UCLA formal diner organizers that Korean-American alumni are concerned about the image and empowerment of the Korean-American community at UCLA and in the Los Angeles context.

Another way to do it is a more subtle way. Here, the use of a key signifier can be effective. Let us suppose that every alumni are given a moment to speak. She can stand up and say, "I am a 1.5 generation Korean-American and I have seen and experienced a lot. I have learned a lot as a 1.5 Korean-American student at UCLA. And I believe that we 1.5 Korean-Americans should contribute to UCLA in significant ways. 1.5 Korean-Americans have created many of the Korean-American groups at UCLA, and I know that we can help UCLA in significant ways in the future." The fact that she is using 1.5 over and over again will raise flags in the minds of Korean-Americans attending the dinner. She could have used the term "Korean-American" without the prefix "1.5" or "1.5 generation." The blatant use of the term will make Korean-Americans uncomfortable, and their remembrance of their painful immigration experience will be heightened. "1.5" stands for the painful integration and clash of two cultures – Korean and American.

If this Korean-American woman thought that the white mayor deliberately ignored the Korean-American community, then it is more than likely that other Korean-American alumni would have felt the same thing. They would have been equally sensitive to UCLA's ignoring this problem. However, without a direct action or a key signifier, these Korean-American alumni may have contributed $100,000 each to the general UCLA scholarship fund with the aggregate contribution in the millions.

But a direct appeal or a key signifier will cause them to hesitate and even stop their contribution. The message being sent by the key signifier of "1.5 generation" is that Korean-Americans must be cautious about whites and act in a pro-Korean way. This message has the concrete result of hindering any kind of support of whites in the context of UCLA. They would not want to support anything that would make Korean-Americans invisible at UCLA or Los Angeles and only make whites shine. There is a direct impact to the use of "1.5" or "1.5 generation".

"1.5 generation" is a key signifier because it recalls the semantic field of collective memory of the Korean-American population. Furthermore, it propels an anti-white stand/action and a pro-Korean stand/action. This is possible because of what the term "1.5 generation" represents within the internal discourse of the Korean-American community. Furthermore, in the collective memory, 1.5 generation of Koreans have been tied to the struggle of Koreans to empower themselves in strongly white contexts, such as the Ivy League. The key signifier would not have any impact on the white population sitting at the fund-raising dinner. They would not know what meaning is conveyed and what action is called for.

Of course, if they read this book, they will understand. But even if they cognitively understand, "1.5" will not have any impact on them personally or affect their action if they are not Korean-Americans. "1.5" has an impact on Korean-Americans present because it is a part of their collective-memory, which is personally important to them and has a bearing on their understanding of the self, their community, and their place in it.

Indeed, the key signifier is significant because of its associated value to the semantic and experiential world of collective memory and community value. Without this relationship, the trigger function would not work. And to understand the workings of the triggering function, the academic must pursue an indepth study into the history and socio-cultural experience of the community under investigation.

Every community has key signifiers. Often, we do not critically try to assess what they are. Sometimes, we use key signifiers functionally without dissecting the nature or method of usage. But key signifiers, when correctly identified, can open worlds to us in ways that other literary devices cannot. What we cannot see in a simile or in a metaphor, we can see in a key signifier. It is far more difficult to identify key signifiers and much more study is required to identify them. But in the long-run, it is far more rewarding on an intellectual level. When done properly, key signifiers can encapsulate the hopes and fears of a community in a single word or a phrase.

Having discussed the nature of the double-layer trigger function of key signifiers at length, I would like to explain the nature of the impact on the audience. As already mentioned, the key signifier really only impacts the in-group. In other words, the key signifier is meaningful only for those who share in the collective memory or community value. Those who are not in the in-group will not be affected by it, whereas the key signifier will prompt in-group members to concrete action.

Thus, it is possible for 200 people to be sitting at the alumni formal dinner of UCLA Alumni Association with the Los Angeles Mayor as the guest speaker, but only the Korean-Americans in the group will be affected by the use of the key signifier of "1.5 generation." In other words, although 200 people are sitting in the same room and hearing the same mini-speech, only the Korean-Americans in the room – say, around 30 – are impacted by the key signifier. In a way, this is the power of the key signifier. It is like the smart bomb of literary devices.

Thus, in a given setting it is possible to explain the nature of the impact on the audience – by key signifiers – as divided into effectual impact for the in-group members who share collective memory or community value and the intended non-impact for the outsiders or those not in the in-group.

Of course, it is possible for 100 per cent of the audience to be members of the in-group. For instance, it is possible for a Korean-American to give a speech using the term "1.5 generation" in a formal dinner of the alumni of the Korean-American Students Association at UCLA. All the Korean-Americans present can receive the impact intended by the key signifier. If there are no white people present and only Korean-Americans are present, then the key signifier can impact 100 per cent of the audience. So, the audience is not necessarily divided into in-group and out-group.

It is important, however, to recognize the potential of the in-group and out-group division. Even if we use the example of alcohol and Fundamentalist Christianity, this would apply. It is possible for Rev. Billy Graham to address a room that is 100 per cent Fundamentalist Christians, who share the same value that consumption of alcohol is wrong and not compatible with holy Christian living. In this context, the impact of using a key signifier related to the prohibition of alcohol would be more or less 100 per cent, since the audience is all Fundamentalist Christian.

However, if Rev. Billy Graham were preaching at a Billy Graham Crusade, where there are some Fundamentalist Christians, but many who would not describe themselves as such, the key signifier attached to prohibition of alcohol consumption would most likely be missed by non-Fundamentalist Christians. In regards to alcohol and Fundamentalist Christianity, they are outsiders and not in the in-group to which Rev. Billy Graham belongs. In fact, studies after studies show that many non-Christians attend Billy Graham Crusades.

A key signifier has an intended audience. And the intended audience must share a common collective memory or a community value. If they do not, the double-layered trigger mechanism cannot work. A key signifier that does not trigger the past and trigger an action (in a way, we can speak about this in terms of "future") is not a key signifier at all. The key signifier must accomplish both parts of the function associated with its identity.

Throughout this book, examples after examples will help clarify the nature of key signifiers and their function in a particular context. Key signifiers, like simile and metaphor, are everywhere. Often, people use them even without thinking about them.

But just like the simile and the metaphor, the key signifier deserves critical study. This book coins the term, defines it, and describes its nature and function. Hopefully, this book will increase the appreciation of the key signifier as a literary device. Proper appreciation of key signifiers will open up semantic and experiential worlds in ways other literary devices will not allow.

Chapter 2

Key Signifiers in the Bible

Key signifier is a literary device and can be detected in written texts as well as in spoken speech. Just as one can use a simile or a metaphor in writing and speaking, one can use a key signifier in writing and speech. The Bible clearly shows the use of simile and metaphor; thus, simply reading through the Bible will give ample examples. Likewise, there are many attestations of key signifiers in the Bible.

In this chapter, I will discuss how the Bible uses the literary device of the key signifier. My thinking about this topic was spurred when I participated in teaching a course entitled "Bible as Literature" to undergraduates at Brown University in Providence, Rhode Island, during the 1998-1999 academic year. Because the Bible is a written text, it can be studied in light of linguistic tools and literary devices that are a part of that written text. Even the most devoutly religious person would not object to identifying simile and metaphor in the Bible. They exist. In the same way, key signifiers exist. They are used as literary devices.

The best way to approach the question of identifying key signifiers in the Bible and understanding them is through examples. The example I have chosen comes from the Gospel according to Mark 6:14-29. This pericope is generally referred to as "The Beheading of John the Baptist." Pericope is a term used by New Testament scholars to refer to the smallest literary unit in the Gospels that coheres together. The pericope is like a mini-story or a mini-event with a beginning, a middle, and an end. Thus, it is possible to talk about the Gospel as a string of perciopes. You can take out any of the pericopes from the Gospels and they should be able to stand alone as a whole story – albeit a min-whole story.

Mark 6:14-19 describes the account of how John the Baptist was beheaded. Before identifying and discussing the key signifier in this Gospel pericope, it would be helpful to summarize the pericope. The Markan pericope starts with King Herod hearing about the fame of Jesus Christ, whom some were beginning to say was John the Baptist raised from the dead. The story unfolds and soon we find out in the pericope that Herod had John the Bapist beheaded and that is why he was concerned at the rumors about Jesus of Nazareth. This is the introduction to the pericope.

The body of the story relates how it came to be that Herod beheaded John the Baptist. In the body of the Gospel pericope, we find out that Herod did not intend to behead John the Baptist. King Herod merely had John the Baptist arrested and put in prison to silence him in public because John the Baptist kept condemning King Herod for marrying Herodias, his brother Philip's wife.

The condemnation of the marriage to King Herod understandably angered the wife – Herodias, who had been the wife of King Herod's brother Philip. She had a grudge against John the Baptist and wanted to have him killed. But Herodias could not bring about the death of John the Baptist because King Herod protected him. The Markan pericope shows that King Herod believed John the Baptist to be righteous and a holy man. So, King Herod liked to listen to John the Baptist preach, although his sermons confused him.

While John the Baptist was in King Herod's prison, King Herod threw a big banquet for his high government officials, military commanders, and elites of Galilee. During the banquet, Herodias' daughter (presumably the daughter from the previous marriage to Philip, King Herod's brother) danced for King Herod and his guests.

King Herod and his guests were pleased with the dancing. The king was so pleased that he told Herodias' daughter to ask for whatever she wanted, and he promised to give her anything she wanted "up to half of my kingdom" (Mark 6:23).

When King Herod made such a generous offer, Herodias' daughter went out to her mother and asked her what she should request from the king. Herodias, who had been looking for an opportunity to kill John the Baptist, told her daughter to request the head of the John the Baptist. Herodias' daughter went back to the king and his guests and requested the head of John the Baptist on a platter.

King Herod was upset by this request because he respected John the Baptist, but because he had made a promise with an oath and because he did so in front of his honored guests, he did not want to deny her request. So, King Herod sent an order to have an executioner behead John the Baptist and bring his head. When the head of John the Baptist was brought and given to Herodias' daughter, she gave it to her mother. The body of the story ends there. And the Mark 6:14-29 pericope ends with a concluding remark that John the Baptist's disciples came and took his body and buried him in a tomb.

This pericope is a very important part of the Gospel story as a whole. In the Gospel tradition, John the Baptist is represented as the chief precursor to Jesus Christ, who in fact had been chosen by God to pave the way for Christ's coming (Mark 1:1-8). Thus, it can be argued that this pericope represents a peak of the Gospel according to Mark. Because this pericope is significant in the larger context of the Gospel according to Mark, any key signifier found in this pericope would be significant to the whole of the Gospel according to Mark.

What is the key signifier found in the Mark 6:14-29 pericope? The key signifier is "up to half my kingdom" in verse 23. As we have discussed, key signifier necessarily triggers collective memory or community value. The semantic and experiential field being triggered from the past (or present) has to be significant enough that all in the in-group can be "triggered" by the key signifier.

In the case of the key signifier of "up to half my kingdom" found in Mark 6:23, the case proves to be true. The key signifier, "up to half my kingdom," is found in the Book of Esther in the Old Testament. Not only is the Book of Esther a major book of the canonized Old Testament, which the audience of the Gospel of Mark would have taken to be authoritative scripture, there was an active annual celebration attached to the Book of Esther – namely, Purim.

According to the Book of Esther 9:21, Jews were to celebrate the festival of Purim on the fourteenth and fifteenth days of the month of Adar. Generally, this falls during the month of April. Since the month of Adar in the Jewish calendar is based on the lunar cycle, it differs from our calendar. So, although fourteenth and fifteenth day of the month of Adar is fixed in the lunar calendar, it is has no fixed date on the solar calendar system.

Jews around the world who are remotely religious still celebrate Purim as a major religious holiday. This was the case at the time of Jesus Christ and the time of the composition of the Gospel of Mark. Thus, everyone would have related to and be potentially impacted by the key signifier of "up to half my kingdom" in Mark 6:23 which draws on the Purim tradition and the Book of Esther.

As many of the readers will not be familiar with Purim or the Book of Esther in great detail, it is important to summarize the story of Esther. This way it would be easier to explain how the key signifier of "up to half my kingdom" in Mark 6:23 can trigger the semantic and experiential field of collective memory and community value founded in Purim and the Book of Esther.

The story of Esther takes place in the Diaspora in the modern-day Iran, when the ancient empire of Persia reigned supreme in the region. King Xerxes was the ruler of the land and the story is basically a story based on courtly intrigue. The story begins with King Xerxes showcasing his wealth and opulence and throwing lavish parties for his nobility. Drunk on wine, King Xerxes commands his seven eunuchs to bring his Queen Vashti to display her before his party guests in her royal splendor. But when the eunuchs delivered the king's command, Queen Vashti refused to come. Like a pouting, drunk frat-boy, the King becomes very angry. And he consults his legal advisors.

He asks them what should be done to Queen Vashti according to the law for disobeying the king's command. Memucan, one of the seven trusted nobles of Persia consulted, did not speak from the stand-point of law but from the practical implications for the nobles. Memucan's argument was that if Queen Vashti was allowed to have the free will not to come when her husband beckons, then the wives of the nobles will develop a sense of women's liberation and act on their own free will and may choose not to come when they are summoned by their husbands. For this primary reason to keep women down in the Persian Empire, Memucan suggested making a royal decree kicking Queen Vashti out of her place of honor and not allowing her to ever appear before the King. King Xerxes listens to Memucan and issues the decree as Memucan proposed.

After some time passed, King Xerxes's hot temper subsided. He remembered the decree he had issued against Queen Vashti, whose beauty he appreciated. Noticing his resolve wavering, king's personal attendants proposed having a beauty contest throughout the Persian Empire for the most beautiful virgins in King Xerxes' realm. Winners will join King's harem at the citadel of Susa and be groomed with beauty treatments by Hegai, one of the eunuchs of the king who was in charge of beautifying the harem virgin girls to maximize the king's pleasure as he deflowered them. The girl who gratifies King Xerxes the most in the deflowering process gets the title of the Queen.

There was a Jew, named Mordecai, from the tribe of Benjamin in the citadel of Susa, who had been carried into exile in Babylon by King Nebuchadnezzar among other Jews who were taken captive along with King Johoiachin, the king of Judah. Life in exile was hard. There were many orphans and widows. Hadassah was an orphan cousin of Mordecai, whom he adopted as his own daughter and raised in the exile. Hadassah had a Persian name and it was Esther. Esther was very pretty.

When Mordecai found out about the beauty pageant for pretty virgins to win the opportunity to be deflowered by the Persian king and join his harem and have the chance to win the ultimate prize of becoming his queen, he thought of his adopted daughter, who was the daughter of his uncle Abihail. Esther was beautiful, and she was a virgin. She satisfied the criteria for the beauty pageant. Being a part of the sex-family of King Xerxes would bring many pleasures. She would not have to worry about food or clothing. And she would have a relatively comfortable life. Life in exile was hard, and Mordecai decided that being a sex partner of the Persian king was better than living in poverty as a Jew.

After entering Esther in the sex context for King Xerxes, Mordecai made Esther promise him not to tell anyone that she was a Jew. Since Jews were exiles and a conquered people, Mordecai thought this could disadvantage Esther from joining the king's harem. Esther became a finalist and had the opportunity to lose her virginity to King Xerxes of the Persian Empire. She took the advice of Hegai, who knew about such things and the tastes of the Persian king, and Esther managed to win the first prize of being the Queen.

Mordecai, who lived a hard life in the exile as a semi-vagrant, happened to be sitting at the king's gate and heard the plot by two of the king's body guards, Bigthana and Teresh, to assassinate the king. Mordecai was not going to miss his opportunity to give his adopted daughter the opportunity to protect her new position and court favor with the court. So, he passed the word to her. She told the king and gave credit to Mordecai. The king checked the story out, found it to be true, and then killed the two body guards. This episode was written down in the royal annals.

King Xerxes did not do anything for Mordecai, who had revealed the plot to Esther. Mordecai was sore from this, and to add insult to injury, King Xerxes elevated someone else. King Xerxes honored Haman, who was already a noble, but gave him a position above all the other nobles. King Xerxes ordered everyone to bow down and give honor to Haman.

Mordecai, angry at the king for not giving him some reward for saving his life and jealous at Haman for receiving all the honors, refused to obey the king's command. There was no religious prohibition to honoring Haman; it was just a matter of wounded pride and personal jealousy. The royal officials saw that Mordecai did not obey the king's command to honor Haman, so they approached him and asked him the legitimate question of why he was not complying with the king's command. Day after day, Mordecai refused to obey the king's order to honor Haman. And just to spite them, he told them that he was a Jew, like it was for some kind of a nationalistic reason.

The royal officials told Haman about it, just to see what the newly elevate *primus inter pares* noble would do. Egged on by royal officials, Haman came to pay attention to the fact that Mordecai did not show him honor. After a while, Haman's grudge against Mordecai grew, and he wanted to kill him. And being spurred on by royal officials, Haman wanted to kill not only Mordecai, but his people.

Haman being the bright noble that he was did some research and found out what kind of people the Jews were. Persian Empire being a great empire had all kinds of people in its realm. With his newly gained knowledge, Haman approached King Xerxes and told him about a people scattered throughout his empire who posed a threat to national security. These Jews did not respect the national customs and were different from the majority of the populace. Haman asked the king for permission to destroy the national threat and bring money into the national coffers. After all, when the Jews are killed, their possessions could be confiscated. Haman would take a cut and hand out necessary cuts for those involved, and he could place a significant sum of money into king's national treasures. Like any ruler, the idea of fattening national treasury attracted King

Xerxes. And the argument from national security appealed to him as well. So, King Xerxes gave the go ahead for Haman to put a program of destroying Jews in the name of national security and interest. But seeing that national security was a serious issue and recognizing that the newly formed Homeland Security Department needed funds, King Xerxes told Haman to keep the money to use to execute his program to neutralize the national threat that Jews posed. After all, the Persian Empire was a rich country, but they worried constantly about national security because there were many terrorists and nations that looked for an opportunity to attack.

With the official national approval for his private war, Haman went about executing Jews at will. Haman had access to all the security forces, governors, local officials, and the police force on a local, state, and federal levels to carry out his program in the name of national security.

When Mordecai heard of this, he went around the city crying loudly and bitterly while tearing his clothing like a crazy man. Mordecai knew that it was because of his jealousy for Haman and personal grudge against the king that this was happening. Out of personal guilt and also to show other Jews that he was a good Jew who wailed to God in the manner expected of religious Jews in times of crisis, he went around crying out loud. Walking like a crazy man in the concentrated public area among people whom he knew also served the function of protecting him from Haman, who started this whole thing because of Mordecai and his hatred for him and desire to kill him.

Esther hearing of her step-father acting like a crazy-man, tearing his clothes and crying out loud, sent her maids and eunuchs to find out what was wrong. Mordecai was not going to lose the opportunity to get the Queen on his side and told her everything that was happening against Jews. Haman had set a date to kill all the Jews in the Persian Empire via various government and social agencies in the empire. Of course, Mordecai left out the part about how he broke the king's edict out of personal spite and jealousy, which resulted in the annihilation program against the Jews.

Esther sent back message to Mordecai that she was afraid to go to the king because all who go without being summoned would be killed. There was one exception – if the king extended the golden sceptre. But this was not a sure thing. And Esther knew what happened to her predecessor. Being a smart woman, she knew that King Xerxes had it in him to replace her as well.

Mordecai noticed that Esther was trying to save her own skin. So, Mordecai threatened her and said that even she would die because of the annihilationist program against Jews. It was probably not true, but Mordecai's threat was credible to Esther. Being afraid for her life and thinking that she would be annihilated, too, Esther resolved to go to the king. Esther asked Mordecai to gather all the Jews in Susa and have them fast and pray for her for 3 days. Esther said that she would take her chance of being destroyed completely.

Queen Esther took her best royal clothes, prettied herself, and went to the king. King Xerxes extended the golden sceptre and received his queen. Queen Esther looked absolutely ravishing and the king's weakness as a man took over. Impulsively, King Xerxes asked what she wanted and promised to give her what she wanted even "up to half the kingdom" (Esther 5:3).

Esther did not tell King Xerxes what she wanted right away. Instead, she invited the king and Haman to a banquet. King Xerxes summoned Haman, and they attended Esther's banquet, that day. At the banquet, in the presence of Haman, the king again asked Esther what she wanted. Again, King Xerxes promised that he would grant her request even "up to half the kingdom" (Esther 5:6).

Of course, the reader or listener knows at this point what Esther really wants. She wants the head of Haman on a platter to save Jews. But again Esther does not answer the king with the expected answer. She again invited the king and Haman for a banquet for the next day. By this time in the narrative, "up to half the kingdom" has become formulaic. The king asks what the request is. The reader or listener is expecting a reply from Esther that she does not give. Esther keeps egging on the king and the readers. "Up to half the kingdom" keeps ringing in the listener's ears. The reader is tempted to shout: "Just tell him what you want, Esther! You want Haman's head on a platter!" But in terms of narrative, the suspense works. And in the process, "up to half the kingdom" becomes coined and minted in the collective memory.

After the first banquet, Haman is elated. He thinks that the world is going his way. Not only was he invited to one banquet that was a private affair with the king and the queen, now he's invited to another private banquet with the king and the queen. This stroked his ego and put him off his guard. As Haman was in the habit of seeing Mordecai on a daily basis, he saw Mordecai again. And the combination of elation from the banquet and his newly gained sense of greater self-importance fuelled his anger further when Mordecai as usual refused to show him respect as was required by the king's edict.

When Haman saw his friends, he bragged about the private party that Queen Esther threw for him and the king. And he did more bragging about his self-importance. And he added that Modecai was a thorn in the side because he loitered about in the king's gate and refused to show respect as required by law. Haman's wife Zeresh suggested building a gallows 75 feet high and asking the king in the morning to have Mordecai hanged on it. Then, he can go to the private dinner banquet, happily. Haman liked his wife's idea, so he decided to follow the program.

Unfortunately for Haman, King Xerxes had a sleepless night. He, in fact, was bored and asked his attendants to bring the royal annals to him to be read. He was reminded that a certain Mordecai had exposed Bigthana and Teresh, two of his body guards who were planning to assassinate him. The king asked if Mordecai received honor for saving his life. When King Xerxes found out that he did not, he asked about any advisors who may be at the court at the time. Haman was there to ask the king to allow him to hang Mordecai. He really did not need the permission to do this because he already had permission from the king to kill all the Jews, but it was his wife's idea and he had a lapse of memory.

In a twist of irony, his unnecessary search for permission ended up giving Mordecai honor, rather than death. The king asked Haman what should be done for a man that "king delights to honor." At such a generic question, Haman naturally assumed that the king was talking about him. After all, he had been singled out to be the greatest and the most honored noble in the land. And he had just been to a private dinner banquet thrown by Queen Esther. And that very night, he was going to another private dinner banquet, just with the king and the queen. Who else could it be?

So, Haman went on and on about the greatest honor that a person could possibly receive, such as wearing royal clothing, riding on animals fit for royalty, and being accompanied by royalty and nobility in a festive procession throughout the land with a prince shouting, "This is what the king does for someone whom he really likes!"

Haman thought of the greatest honor possible from his wildest fantasy because he thought it was for him. But ironically, it was applied to Mordecai. And what could he do but carry out the king's command? Humiliated, Haman returned home and told his wife and friends what had happened to him that day. Haman's wife gives him advice again. This time, she gives him a completely opposite advice. Zeresh tells Haman not to stand against Mordecai because he was his bad luck. She thought that standing against him would bring him ruin.

At that time, Hamaan's ride for the private banquet thrown by Queen Esther arrived. Disoriented and confused, Mordecai was not quite himself when he went to the banquet. At the banquet, the king asks the expected question and gives the expected promise. He would give whatever Esther asked even "up to half the kingdom" (Esther 7:2). This time, Queen Esther gives the expected reply.

Esther asks the king to spare her people, who had been "sold" for slaughter and annihilation. King Xerxes asks who did such a thing. Esther replied that it was Haman. King Xerxes became very angry. It must have been a mixture of emotions. He did not know that Esther was a Jew, and perhaps before that day did not care. And he felt a sense of guilt because it was he who had signed the executive order to allow Haman to "sell" Esther's people to slaughter and annihilation. King Xerxes needed to clear his mind, so he went off into the garden.

Haman became afraid. And he was not thinking rationally because of all the events of the day. So, he plunged toward Queen Esther to seek her mercy and to have her speak on his behalf to the king. In his right mind, Haman would have known that it's never a good idea to be caught in close proximity to a woman when her lover is very angry. When King Xerxes returned, he saw Haman physically near Esther practically touching her and in an emotional supplication.

King Xerxes accused Haman of trying to molest the queen. He read things in sexual terms like a typical man. Whereas the king could have done something rational, the scene of another man being so near his woman made him feel jealous and he reacted in an extreme way. As the king was in a state of anger, one of the king's eunuchs who probably bore a grudge against Haman for all the honors he had received from the king informed King Xerxes in a timely manner that Hamaan had built a gallows that is 75 feet high and that it was built for Mordecai, who had saved the king's life. This was the straw that broke the camel's back. The king ordered that Haman be immediately hanged on it.

King Xerxes gave Esther the estate of Haman. And learning of Mordecai's relationship to Esther and remembering that he had saved his life, King Xerxes gave Mordecai Haman's ring and honors. Seeing that King Xerxes was under her female power, Esther piled on her feminine charm. She started to cry and weep and beg the King to end the plan that Haman had placed in motion against the Jews.

Overcome by her feminine wiles, King Xerxes gave Mordecai a blank check to do as he wanted and create a law which he saw fit. Mordecai annulled Haman's edicts against the Jews, and put in its place similarly violent edicts against the enemies of Jews. Thus, whereas Haman wanted to annihilate the Jews and take their property, Mordecai sealed with the king's seal the edict throughout the empire the right of Jews to annihilate their enemies and take their property at will. Mordecai had at his disposal local, state, and federal police force. And as the head of Home Land Security endowed with emergency executive powers, Mordecai ordered all the local, state, and federal leaders to assist Jews in annihilating whomever they deemed to be their enemy. Many in the Persian Empire converted to Judaism because they were afraid of the new violent edict.

The book of Esther recounts the execution of the edict. Jews went around with government authority to annihilate any people they called their enemy and took their property. And they celebrated their violence and murder in a religious ceremony that came to be referred to as Purim. And Purim was to be celebrated every year from that day onwards. Because of the regular celebration of Purim and because the book of Esther was a part of the scriptural canon, it is not difficult to see the function of the Book of Esther and the Purim tradition on the collective memory and community value of Jews at the time of Jesus Christ and the writing of the Gospel according to Mark.

Having recounted the story of the book of Esther and Purim at length, we can now begin to discuss how all this fit together to help us better understand the function of the key signifier found in Mark 6:14-29. Let us start by asking the question: How does the key signifier of "up to half my kingdom" in Mark 6:23 function as a key signifier vis-à-vis the collective memory of Purim?

On a simplistic level, this is quite easy to answer. We have noticed that there are three places that this very phrase is mentioned in the book of Esther – Esther 5:3, Esther 5:6, and Esther 7:2. The very phrase "up to half my kingdom" would have been associated with the book of Esther and Purim. It is important to remember that Purim was celebrated annually, and often the book of Esther was read in conjunction with the celebration of Purim. This means that a religious Jew at the time of Jesus of Nazareth would have heard the reading of the book of Esther at least once per year and every year. It is not unlike the Christmas story. A religious Christian will hear the Gospel account about the birth of Jesus Christ at least once every year at Christmas time. In this way, Purim is to Jews what Christmas is to Christians. Since the portions of Esther containing the phrase "up to half my kingdom" were a part of the central part of the book of Esther, the phrase would have received much attention.

Perhaps, this example will help clarify the impact of the key signifier, "up to half of my kingdom." Think now in the Christian context of Christmas. Christians have read and heard Christmas story so often in the Gospels, that if someone were to say, "Peace on earth and good will to men," Christians would immediately associate it with the Christmas story found in the Gospels. This is because Christians have heard this phrase often and even perhaps every Christmas in the context of the celebration of Christmas. It has become a part of the Christian collective memory. In the same way, "up to half of my kingdom" became an integral part of Jewish collective memory because Purim was celebrated every year and the book of Esther normally read.

Thus, if someone said, "up to half my kingdom" not specifically in the Purim celebration context, most people would understand that it's a saying from the book of Esther and associated with Purim. Thus, it will remind the listener or reader of its original context. To elaborate on this point, let us suppose that a certain Joshua at the time of Jesus of Nazareth said, "I love her so much that I would give her up to half my kingdom." His listeners would immediately associate the saying with the story in the book of Esther. This is a strong way of saying that Joshua loves this woman very strongly. His Jewish listeners will recall that this saying is associated with King Xerxes killing his best advisor, Haman, the one whom he had given the greatest honors and elevated over all other nobles in the Persian empire. King Xerxes' love for Esther was so great that he was willing to kill his best friend and turn his back on his people and give the Jews the right to annihilate anyone they felt like by royal decree and with the use of governmental and police agencies.

In this regard, saying "I love her so much that I would give up to half my kingdom" would be far more powerful than saying, "I love her so much that I would give up my whole kingdom for her." The latter saying does not have any associative significance for the Jews of Jesus of Nazareth's time. It doesn't imply that the speaker is willing to betray his best friend for the woman. It doesn't imply that he is willing to have all his people subject to potential annihilation for the woman. The first saying with the key signifier "up to half my kingdom" has that semantic referent built into the collective memory of the Jews at Jesus Christ's time.

In other words, the phrase "up to half my kingdom" has a powerful meaning and usage because of its original usage. It would have been impossible for a Jew in Jesus Christ's time to use the phrase "up to half my kingdom" without recalling the book of Esther and the story of Purim. It is like when Christians say, "Peace on earth and good will to men." It is impossible for a Christian not to remember that this was a saying originally in the context of the birth of Jesus Christ. This would be the case whether the speaker was saying this in the context of a sermon at a Christian church or if a politician were saying this in the context of his campaign speech.

Suppose that someone running for the Senate position of New York State said, "We have to strive for peace on earth and good will toward men. And I pledge to fight to achieve this if you vote me to be your Senator." It will be impossible for Christians in the room not to associate this saying with the birth narrative of Jesus of Nazareth. The semantic world of the Gospel story will be recalled by Christian listeners. And images of messianic deliverance will be playing around in the subconscious. Most Christians will understand that the candidate for the position of New York Senator is pledging to be a savior figure. The phrase will have a greater impact on Christians because of what they associate that phrase to be – clearly tied to the Christmas story.

It is important to stress that just as Christians cannot but associate "peace on earth, good will to men" with Christmas, Jews in Jesus Christ's time could not but associate "up to half my kingdom" with the book of Esther and the Purim tradition. Every Jew in Jesus Christ's time knew that the book of Esther was a triumphal tract extolling the Jews and the Jewish right to annihilate their enemies and take their possessions. In this regard, the phrase "up to half my kingdom" would have been a type of code phrase to fuel Jewish nationalism and militancy.

Thus, as a key signifier for Jewish communities both in Israel and throughout the Jewish Diaspora, "up to half my kingdom" would have been meant to incite Jewish loyalty and Jewish pride. The key signifier would spur anti-Gentile militancy and actions. In a way, it would have been a trigger mechanism to incite Jews against those who opposed the Jewish community. That is why it is so interesting to find this important Jewish key signifier in the Mark 6:14-29 pericope.

Let us compare the context of the use of the key signifier in the Gospel pericope and in the book of Esther. We notice that the context is similar. In both contexts, the ruler of the land promises "up to half the kingdom" to a woman who has found favor in his eyes. In the Markan pericope, it is the daughter of Herodias who has found favor in the eyes of King Herod. In the book of Esther it is Esther, whose Jewish name was Hadassah, who has found favor in the eyes of King Xerxes.

But there are some differences as well. Whereas in the book of Esther, Esther is the wife of King Xerxes who legitimately deserves such a great favor from her husband, in the Markan pericope, it is not the wife of King Herod, but rather her daughter from the previous marriage. It is inappropriate for King Herod to promise up to half the kingdom to someone who is not his wife. What adds to this notion is the fact that he promises such a great thing after he delights in her dancing for him and his guests. What is understood in this context is the idea that there is some kind of inappropriate tie between King Herod and his step-daughter. What fuels this perception is the fact that King Herod is portrayed as an unscrupulous individual when it comes to sexual relations. King Herod married his brother Philip's wife, which John the Baptist condemned. It was for this reason why he was imprisoned. The Christian text seems to have an agenda to portray the Jewish king as immoral and capable of any kind of sexual transgression. If King Herod can marry the wife of his brother, then, of course, he could engage in sexual relations with his step daughter. The fact that he is drunk on wine as Herodias' daughter dances for him recalls the event of Lot being drunk when his daughters seduce him to have sex with them (Genesis 19:30-38).

What makes the dubious relationship between King Herod and Herodias' daughter more problematic is that it seems that Herodias is involved in the illicit sexual relations of her daughter and her husband. When King Herod asks Herodias' daughter what she wants and promises her up to half of his kingdom, instead of answering her stepfather, she runs off to her mother. The Markan pericope portrays Herodias as harboring a great hatred of John the Baptist for criticizing her social-climbing marriage to the king. Herodias wanted to have John the Baptist killed, but could not bring this about despite her charms on King Herod. Thus, it is understandable for Herodias to put her daughter up to the plot to get John the Baptist killed. If Herodias could not convince King Herod with all her sexual charms, maybe her daughter could get what she desired the most on her behalf. A woman putting up a surrogate to get what she wants is not unprecedented in the Jewish tradition. In fact, Sarah had put up her most trusted female companion, Hagar, to get what she desired the most, an heir for herself and Abraham (Genesis 16:1-4). This scenario seems to fit the early Christian condemnation of incest. I Corinthians 5:1-2 condemns a man having sex with his stepmother. Daughter of Herodias having sex with her stepfather is the equivalent kind of sexual immorality condemned in 1 Corinthians.

On one level, the Markan pericope can be seen as a direct attack on Judaism. Judaism was not as guarded as Christianity about sexual immorality or incest, at least in the minds of early Christians. Judaism actually required the brother to marry the wife of his brother if he died without leaving an heir. This reality is described in Mark 12:18-23. The Sadducees came to question Jesus Christ about resurrection. In the process they described the Mosaic Law which demands that in the case that the brother dies without having an heir by his wife, the living brother of must marry his brother's widow and have an heir by her. The kind of relation that Judaism allowed and even required was, in fact, what John the Baptist condemned and was jailed for. The Mark 6:14-29 pericope is, therefore, a picture into the Jewish-Christian conflict.

Although the book of Esther and the Mark 6:14-29 pericope differed in terms of the position of the female protagonist, there is also congruence as well. Let me explain this point. It is true that Esther was the legitimate wife of King Xerxes, and Jews generally describe her as a hero, who saved her people. But when we read the book of Esther more closely and think about what Esther did in light of Judaism and its requirements as a whole, Esther does not come off being a saint either. Esther basically entered the depraved context to have her virginity deprived by a Gentile, albeit a king, who was not her husband at the time of the deprivation of her virginity (in the context of the harem). This was expressly forbidden in Judaism. Jews were to marry Jews. And entering the king's harem without knowing for sure she would be his wife (or the queen) was tantamount to selling herself into a type of prostitution. In a sense, Esther engaged in sexual immorality. In this regard, Esther and the daughter of Herodias are similar. Herodias' daughter having sex with her stepfather would have been like someone in a king's harem having sex with the king on one level. This would have been perceived as immoral. Thus, we can conclude that despite some obvious differences there are subtle similarities between the two female protagonists who receive the offer to be given up to half the kingdom.

What other similarities exist between the book of Esther and the Markan pericope under discussion in terms of the key signifier of "up to half my kingdom"? There is the similarity of the setting of the offer to give "up to half the kingdom." In the Markan pericope, it is in the context of the feast that King Herod throws for his government officials, military officials, and other Jewish elites in the area of Galilee. It is a banquet, a festival event, where wine is flowing. The book of Esther is similar, out of the three offers to give up to the half of the kingdom, King Xerxes asked two of them in the context of a banquet (Esther 5:6 and Esther 7:2). And the other offer, although granted not in the setting of a banquet, is offered in a setting that is a direct prelude to the banquet (Esther 5:3). Thus, in the mind of the reader or the listener, the association would also have been with the banquet that followed.

There are other similarities as well. In both pericopes, there is the authority of the king bound to the offer to give up to half of the kingdom. And the request granted, in fact, is not an easy or a light one in both of the stories. In the Markan pericope, King Herod reluctantly orders the head of John the Baptist on a platter. This is the man whom he enjoyed listening to and respected. In fact, for a long time, it was King Herod who defended John the Baptist's life as Herodias desired and sought to have his life killed.

In the similar manner, the request granted to Esther by King Xerxes was not an easy decision. King Xerxes, in fact, had his most trusted advisor, Haman, whom he honored with many titles, killed in order to keep his word to give Esther up to half of the kingdom. Not only did King Xerxes have his most trusted advisor killed without consulting the nobles of his country as it was customary to do before big decisions, as the book of Esther clearly states (Esther 1:13), King Xerxes put a vagrant man, named Mordecai, on a position close to the throne, primarily on the claim of Esther regarding his family relationship to her. This would have clearly infuriated the nobles of the Persian Empire. At a time when his own body guards were plotting his assassination, King Xerxes was probably endangering his own life and his kingdom through his actions. To add fuel to fire, King Xerxes gave Mordecai *carte blanche* authorization to do whatever he wanted vis-à-vis the enemy of the Jews. The result was that Mordecai passed a royal edict to allow Jews to annihilate whomever they wanted and take the possession of those whom Jews killed. And this was carried out. This must have angered the general population and even motivated hostility towards King Xerxes and his royal family. Thus, in a sense, King Xerxes, too, gave up to half his kingdom.

There are definite similarities between the Markan pericope and the book of Esther. It is almost as if the composer of the Markan pericope had the book of Esther in front of him. But as the book of Esther was so familiar to Jews at the time of Jesus Christ and the Purim celebrated annually as a religious holiday, the composer of the Markan story really did not need to have a written text of the book of Esther in front of him. It was in his memory as it was in the collective memory of those around him. It is easy to see why "up to half my kingdom" could function as a key signifier in this context. The key signifier "up to half my kingdom" would have triggered the semantic and experiential field of the collective memory and community value associated with the book of Esther and the annual celebration of Purim.

But there is one disturbing factor. The composer of the Gospel of Mark does not seem to use the key signifier of "up to half of the kingdom" in the way it was intended or was in vogue among the Jews of Jesus Christ's time. What was the intent of the original key signifier?

Originally, the key signifier of "up to half of the kingdom" was meant to muster Jews into a unity to celebrate Jewish solidarity and the right to annihilate Gentiles and take their wealth and defend the Jewish communities. The key signifier recalled the semantic and experiential field of the collective memory imbedded in the book of Esther and the Purim tradition. "Up to half of the kingdom" celebrated killing of the main enemy of the Jews, in the epitomized personage of Haman. But Haman was the embodiment of the enemy of the Jews, and so any enemy would have been represented as a Haman by Jews who remembered the significance of his death in the key signifier "up to half of the kingdom."

But in the Markan pericope, the key signifier of "up to half of the kingdom" is not used in the way it was originally intended. In fact, we find an inversion or twisting of the key signifier by the Christian writer. Why would he do this? The explanation can be simple enough. Christianity was in conflict with Judaism, and the inversion of the key signifier significant to Jews represents the reality of that conflict.

Before going further, it is important to consider, albeit briefly, the fact of the conflict between Christians and Jews. Christians can be defined on a simple level as followers of Jesus Christ. John the Baptist is a Christian because he was a follower of Jesus Christ. John the Baptist described himself as paving the way for Jesus Christ (Mark 1:1-8). He did this because he was a follower of Jesus of Nazareth. Many Jews decided to abandon Judaism and become followers of Jesus Christ. In other words, they became Christians.

It is understandable why Jews would have had problem with Jesus Christ. He kept winning followers from Judaism, who ended up deserting Judaism in the process. The conflict between Jews and Christians became so severe that Jews passed specific religious laws to condemn Christians. In fact, there is a condemnation of Christians (called "Nazarenes" and heretics) in the 18 Benedictions (otherwise known as the Amidah), which religious Jews are required to recite on a daily basis. It is the current scholarly consensus that at least some of the 18 Benedictions were in place at the time of Jesus of Nazareth, including the injunction against Nazarenes and heretics. In fact, in the Gospel of John, we see that Jews had passed a law to kick out of the synagogue anyone who converted to Christianity (John 9:22 and John 12:42).

This brief description of the reality of conflict between Christians (that is, the followers of Jesus Christ) and Jews at the time of Jesus Christ explains why Christians – even converts from Judaism – would have had problems with certain key signifiers that drew on pro-Jewish semantic and experiential reference points based on Jewish collective memory in order to produce a pro-Jewish effect or action. Thus, it is understandable why Christian writers from the period of the New Testament would invert pro-Jewish key signifiers or twist them. And that's exactly what happened with the Mark 6:14-29 pericope.

In the Markan pericope, the key signifier of "up to half my kingdom" exists. And to an extent, it is used in the way it was originally conceived – in a pro-Jewish way. The Jewish King Herod asked Herodias' daughter what she wanted and he promised to give whatever she wanted "up to half the kingdom." And upon consulting her mother, Herodias' daughter requests the head of John the Baptist on a platter. To this point, we can argue that the key signifier functions in the way it was meant to function – to draw on the semantic and experiential referent point of the collective memory stemming from the book of Esther and the Purim tradition. And even having John the Baptist beheaded can be seen as a triumph of Judaism in the same way Esther requesting that Haman be hanged is a triumph for Jews and Judaism. Not only was John the Baptist a thorn on the side for the Jewish king and his queen, he was an offense to Judaism and religious Jews. John the Baptist pulled people away from Jewish religious centers and was instrumental in converting them to Christianity to be followers of Jesus Christ, whom he himself followed. In a sense, therefore, John the Baptist was the greatest threat to Judaism at the time besides Jesus Christ himself. Along with Jesus Christ, John the Baptist was the enemy of the Jews and Judaism. As such, John the Baptist functioned as a type of a Haman.

Thus, we can argue that the whole episode of beheading of John the Baptist and the key signifier of "up to half the kingdom" function in the way they were meant to function in the Jewish context. However, it would be naïve to stop there. It is true that on a literary level, Jews reading this text would have celebrated the beheading of John the Baptist in the same way they would have revelled at the reading of the hanging of Haman in Purim readings of Esther. But the fact is that the Gospel according to Mark was not written by a Jew for a Jewish audience, primarily. The Gospel of Mark was written by a Christian – that is, a follower of Jesus Christ – for other followers of Christ, primarily, as a historical record of the early Christian communal experience with Jesus Christ.

In this historical light, it would be simply inaccurate to say that the key signifier was intended to function in the way it was originally intended. The Christian writer of the Markan pericope was not interested in soliciting a pro-Jewish sentiment with the effect of arousing a pro-Jewish nationalism or zeal. The Christian writer of this Gospel pericope would not have intended celebration of beheading of John the Baptist, who would have been a Haman figure for the religiously Jewish communities. As a follower of Christ, the writer of the Markan pericope condemned the beheading of John the Baptist. As a Christian, the composer of the Markan account would have agreed with John the Baptist's condemnation of incest and sexual immorality. He was a part of early Christianity which emphasized sexual purity and stricter rules for sex and marriage than Judaism required. As mentioned before, Judaism would have required a brother to marry the widow of his brother to bear an heir on behalf of his brother, Christianity would have condemned such a practice as incest.

Indeed, whereas Jews would have celebrated the beheading of John the Baptist as they exulted in the crucifixion of Jesus Christ who threatened to destroy the Jewish Temple and called himself God, and thereby committing blasphemy against the Jewish religion – both of whom were Haman figures – Christians would have sided with John the Baptist and Jesus Christ. This was not only the case for the listener or reader, but also for the composer and redactor as well. It is historically mandatory, that this fact be computed into the investigation into the key signifier of "up to half my kingdom" as used in the Markan pericope.

A question naturally arises. If the composer of the Markan pericope did not want the key signifier of "up to half my kingdom" to function as a key signifier with its original intent, why use it at all? In a way, we can argue that he was following the example of Jesus Christ in the Sermon on the Mount. He was imbuing the key signifier and its fundamental value with Christian content and implication. To understand this point, it would be helpful to spend some time examining what Jesus of Nazareth did in the Sermon on the Mount.

The Sermon on the Mount is found in Matthew 5-7. The major thing that Jesus of Nazareth did in the Sermon on the Mount is to invert key symbols of Judaism. For instance, Jesus Christ directly attacked the Law of Moses, which was held to be the highest value in Judaism. A good example of this is found in Jesus Christ's teaching on divorce, found in Matthew 5:31-32.

The Law of Moses not only allowed divorce but was quite liberal on it. It was easy for a religious Jew to get a divorce under Mosaic Law. All a husband had to do to divorce his wife was to give her a certificate of divorce. As you can imagine, this created all kinds of abuses. Especially since the Law of Moses did not allow the woman to give the certificate of divorce, it was a law that was unfairly prejudiced against the wife. Even if the husband beat her, cheated on her, or did all kinds of horrible things against his wife, she could not divorce him. In contrast, the husband could divorce his wife at will. If he found a younger, more attractive woman that he liked, all he had to do was give a certificate of divorce to his wife and she had to accept the divorce. The husband could, thus, easily trade in an old wife with a new, younger one. This left many Jewish children "fatherless." It was because of this Mosaic Law, the term "fatherless" became an important part of Jewish discourse at the time and it is certainly found in religious writings at the time.

Besides the unfairness of the woman not being allowed to divorce her husband while he could divorce her on a whim, there were other issues involved. When the husband divorced his wife, he was not really required to give any payment to her. That is why the fatherless are described like orphans in Jewish literature. The woman was left without financial support from the husband who divorced him, and her children were left defenseless. This was a major problem at the time of Jesus of Nazareth.

In this light, it can be explained that Jesus Christ was trying to protect women and their rights by prohibiting divorce. In Matthew 5:31-32, Jesus of Nazareth recognizes the Law of Moses granting the right to every married man to divorce his wife with a certificate of divorce. The understanding is that, like the traditional law, any husband has the fundamental right to divorce his wife on a whim under the Mosaic Law. Recognizing this reality, Jesus Christ condemns divorce and, thereby, stands against the Mosaic Law and the Judaism it represents. Jesus of Nazareth proclaims that any man who divorces his wife except in the case that she cheated on him with another man causes her to become an adulteress. In other words, a man who divorces a wife who is faithful to him for any other reason (like incompatibility) is guilty of the sin of pimping her out as a prostitute. This is a serious charge, but Jesus Christ takes divorce this seriously. One can say that Jesus Christ is trying to protect the right of women. To a large extent, this probably played a major role.

There is a bit of a problem, however. After prohibiting divorcing one's wife except in the case of marital unfaithfulness, Jesus Christ prohibits marrying a divorced woman. A question rises: How could this be helping women's rights? It was probably not the woman's fault that she was divorced. After all, Jewish men were allowed to divorce their wife on a whim. She could be completely innocent and righteous and the fault lies completely with the man who has the sole authority to give the certificate of divorce. There is really no defense for this claim. There were a lot of divorced women. Many of them were unfairly divorced. Why does Jesus Christ prohibit both married men and divorced men from marrying a divorced woman? In fact, Jesus Christ claims that anyone who marries a divorced woman commits adultery. The only possible explanation that I can offer at this point is that Jesus Christ was interested in ending divorce altogether and prohibiting marriage to divorced women while prohibiting men from getting divorced would encourage both men and women to work hard at their marriage and do all they could not to let divorce happen. Many Christians struggle with this passage. But currently, both Fundamentalist Christians and the Roman Catholic Church take this command of Christ very seriously and prohibit divorce as a matter of Christian law.

For the purposes of this book, what is most important about the discussion of divorce found in the Sermon on the Mount is the fact that Jesus Christ directly opposed Judaism and Mosaic Law. It is not surprising why Jewish men would have been very upset by this Christian law which Jesus Christ introduced, which limited their freedom to give out certificate of divorce on a whim. And Jewish religious leaders would have been angered by the direct attack on Judaism and the Law of Moses. It is not surprising, in this regard, why there were so many plots by Jews, both the Jewish masses and Jewish religious leaders, to have Jesus Christ killed.

Jesus Christ inverted and subverted Jewish religious laws. He twisted them. Of course, Jesus Christ did not have to mention the Mosaic Law or other principles of Judaism. Jesus of Nazareth could have just introduced or proclaimed his own principles without mean-spirited attack on Judaism and the Law of Moses. But the fact is Jesus Christ did not leave Judaism and the Mosaic Law alone. He reminded his listeners about them and then he inverted and subverted them in the process of outlining Christian laws. It was a method that Jesus Christ employed. And this method became a part of Christian exegesis and a Christian way of relating to Judaism. It is not surprising, therefore, that the composer of Mark 6:14-29 followed in the subversive tradition of Jesus Christ himself.

Indeed, Mark 6:14-29 represents a type of inversion or subversion of Judaism and Jewish traditions that is more subtle. In fact, I would argue that it represents a highly advanced literary style of inverting Jewish traditions building on the philosophical outlook – or the worldview – of Jesus Christ and his dealing with Judaism and the Mosaic Law. Whereas Jesus Christ directly inverted or subverted Judaism and Mosaic Law, certainly in the examples found in the Sermon on the Mount, the writer of the Markan pericope subverted Judaism and Jewish tradition at a higher level of literary composition. He inverted and subverted one of the key signifiers of Judaism and gave it a Christian twist.

How did he do this? "Up to half my kingdom" epitomized the triumph of Jews in the book of Esther. But in the Markan pericope, it became attached to an act of reluctant cowardice borne out of illicit sexual relations in having a righteous man beheaded. In a sense, we can talk about the complete defilement of the original Jewish key signifier that was one of the most important key signifiers in the Jewish tradition.

Why would the composer of Mark 6:14-29 do this? What would be his motivation? On a simple level, we can say that the composer of the Markan pericope did this to spite the Jews. After all, there was a conflict between Christians and Jews and it was a kind of parochial conflict where emotions ran high. It is not difficult to understand why there would be acts of spite going in both directions and that it could have been an end in itself.

This is true, but I would argue that there is more to it than that. The writer of the Gospels did not write the Gospels merely to spite the Jews, even though there is a lot of blatant anti-Jewish elements in the Gospels. Gospel writers were interested in encapsulating the Christian tradition in their literary work for Christians to enjoy as literature and to remember as an account of their history. As writers and literary figures, Gospel writers were interested in leaving behind works of history or literature that had literary significance as well as recounting the historical account of Jesus Christ and his ministry.

Looked at it with sensitivity to the literary and artistic nature of Gospel writings, it is easy to appreciate the effort and energy place into the Gospel writing by its authors. I would argue that the Mark 6:14-29 pericope testifies to the motivation of its author to produce a work of literature that is aesthetically pleasing on an artistic level and which testifies to the artistry of the composure to use literary devices and techniques and to draw from past literatures and histories.

In this regard, I would argue that it was the intentional motivation of the composer of the Markan pericope to invert the key signifier – perhaps the most important key signifier related to Jewish nationalism – and subjugate it under Christian interests. It was a challenging literary endeavor, and the writer of the Markan pericope took up the challenge.

This is not to deny that the event was historical. Some scholars make the mistake of assuming that highly stylized or literary composition is necessarily fiction. This can be true, but it does not necessarily have to be so. Some of the most wonderful pieces of historical writing utilize complex literary techniques. In the study of history, historians refer to this as historiography – or a way or writing history. History is a work of literature on one level because it uses the written word to describe the events that occurred. Often, history takes on the form of narrative, which is reminiscent of story-telling or even fictional stories. It is important to remember that fine literature and factual history are not mutually exclusive.

But the point must be noted. The writer of the Mark 6:14-29 pericope intentionally engage in the challenging exercise of inverting the key signifier. We know this because this key signifier is missing in other accounts of the same historical event. For instance, the account of beheading of John the Baptist found in the Gospel of Mathew (14:1-12) has basically all the elements found in the corresponding Markan pericope, but it is missing the key signifier "up to half my kingdom." Obviously, the inclusion of the key signifier is distinctive to the Gospel of Mark. It was the composer of the Markan pericope who had the ambitious intent of trying his literary expertise of inverting the key signifier of "up to half the kingdom" as found in the Book of Esther.

Was the composer of the Markan pericope successful? I would argue that he was. No one who read the Markan pericope or heard it read could ever think of the original key signifier of "up to half the kingdom" so important to Judaism in the same way again. It no longer was a positive key signifier recalling a positive Jewish collective memory to produce action toward pro-Jewish nationalism and zeal. The reason that the inversion or subversion was successful was because it came to be attached to a new semantic and experiential field – namely of the collective memory of the martyrdom of John the Baptist.

For Christians, John the Baptist was far more important than Esther or Purim. For one, Christians did not celebrate Purim. It was not a Christian holiday. Christians celebrated Christian holidays and engaged in Christian religious activities, such as the Lord's Supper and Baptism. Even Jewish converts to Christianity came to centralize Christian holidays and Christian rituals. Eventually, Jewish customs tied to the Jewish religion were completely phased out. Certainly, literary works such as the Markan pericope inverting the Jewish key signifier of "up to half the kingdom" played a crucial role in phasing out pro-Jewish elements from early Christian communities.

Jews who converted to Christianity and read the Markan pericope could never celebrate Purim in the same way again. This would have been true for Judaizers who wanted to prioritize Jewish traditions, but were converts to Christianity. If they were true Christians who valued Christianity over all else, how could they clap and celebrate as the key signifier of "up to half the kingdom" is introduced in the reading of the book of Esther in the celebration of Purim? They would have remembered the beheading of John the Baptist by King Herod.

"Up to half the kingdom" opened up the semantic and experiential referent of the beheading of John the Baptist in the collective memory of Christians.

We understand how the Jewish key signifier of "up to half the kingdom" was inverted or subverted in the Markan pericope. We see how "up to half the kingdom" came to take on negative connotation for the early Christian communities. In a sense, we can describe this as being a negative key signifier or inverted key signifier or subverted key signifier. For early Christians, it was important to invert and subvert the key signifier important to Judaism and Jews because there were many Jewish converts to Christianity. Many Jews decided to abandon Judaism and follow Jesus Christ. In fact, the first generation of Christians – those who decided to follow Christ – did so and abandoned Judaism.

These Jewish converts to Christianity were born into households that followed Judaism, but they personally made the decision to follow Jesus Christ and become Christians, which by definition are "followers of Jesus Christ." It is not unlike Korea in the 1880s. Many Koreans became converts to Christianity although they had been born into households that followed Buddhism. Even now, Buddhism is the biggest religion in Korea. Those who decided to become Christians – that is, followers of Jesus Christ – abandoned their family religion of Buddhism. Many Koreans were disowned by their parents because they abandoned their ancestral religion which had been practiced for generations and for generations – in fact, for thousands of years. Early Christians on the Korean peninsula suffered persecution by the government, social ostracization, and even martyrdom. Professor Jai-Keun Choi of Yonsei University in Korea published a new book in 2006, entitled *The Origin of the Roman Catholic Church in Korea: An Examination of Popular and Governmental Responses to Catholic Missions in the Late Chosôn Dynasty*, which details this experience of early Korean Christians.

For early Christians in Palestine, who were struggling with persecution from their families and friends for leaving their ancestral religions and values attached to that religion, they needed all the help they could get. Early Christian writers were aware of this and they consciously inverted important value systems – as Jesus Christ did in the Sermon on the Mount – and used complex literary techniques to subvert traditional Jewish semantic and experiential fields attached to their collective memory and community value – as the subverted key signifier of "up to half my kingdom" in the Mark 6:14-29 pericope shows.

The fact that early Christianity was concerned with detaching new converts to Christianity from their ancestral religion and even from the families which exerted pressure on them on behalf of the ancestral family religion is quite clear. Jesus of Nazareth himself made many attacks on the institution of the family as such in an effort to help early Christian converts cope with the difficulties of being disowned by their families for deciding to follow Jesus Christ and for abandoning the family religion and traditional customs attached to that.

For instance, Gospel of Mark 3:31-35 recounts the story of how Jesus Christ rejected his mother and brothers who arrived to meet him. Jesus of Nazareth was working hard to win more followers and convert people from Judaism. As he was speaking with the crowd, his mother and brothers came all the way from Nazareth. It was not a short journey or an easy one. They waited outside as Jesus of Nazareth spoke to the crowd inside. Wanting to see him because they loved him, Jesus Christ's mother and brothers sent a message inside that they were outside wanting to see him. Jesus Christ does not quickly go outside to see his mother and brothers. And Jesus Christ does not take the opportunity to teach about the importance of honoring one's parents or the wonderful nature of the institution of the family.

What did Jesus Christ do? Jesus of Nazareth addressed the crowd and seized the opportunity to teach them that the institution of the family was not important at all. Jesus Christ was deliberately disrespectful of his mother and his brothers. He kept them waiting as he told the crowd: "Who is my mother and brothers?" This was a clear insult to the mother and the brothers who had travelled long distance to see him. And Jesus of Nazareth answered the question that he himself asked. He said that those who were with him in that crowd were his mother and brothers. And then he added that it was the will of God for them to be there with him and the obedience of this will of God made them his mother and his brothers.

This is a revolutionary teaching. Not only does Jesus Christ oppose the 10 Commandments to honor his parents, he deliberately insults his mother and his brothers, who were standing outside. The messenger who carried the news sent by his mother and his brothers that they were outside, waiting for him, most likely carried the words of Jesus Christ back to his mother and brothers. How do you think that they felt when they heard what Jesus of Nazareth said? They probably felt humiliated, insulted, and hurt. Maybe his mother and brothers sneaked inside to verify whether what the messenger said was true or not. Maybe they were so upset waiting for him and at the news that they just took off. All we know is that the Bible does not indicate that Jesus of Nazareth ever met his mother and his brothers after the news was delivered that they were outside, waiting for him. The assumption is that the meeting did not take place.

Why did Jesus Christ deliberately insult his mother and brothers in public? Why did he disrespect them by not going out to see them? Why did Jesus of Nazareth carry on with his preaching and talk with the group that was gathered to hear him speak? Jesus Christ was concerned to teach the lesson that the family was not important at all. To understand why this teaching was important, it is essential that we remember that for the earliest Christians, to become Christians meant abandoning their ancestral family religion of Judaism. Many would have been disowned, and those who were not disowned suffered greatly in their family context for being followers of Jesus Christ. They needed an encouragement to be faithful as new converts to Christianity. Thus, Jesus Christ showed from the example of his own family that being Christian was worth it all. If Jesus Christ took off to meet his mother and brothers eagerly, that would have discouraged his followers, many of whom were abandoned by their families for being Christians.

Some may have renounced their new Christian faith as a result. Jesus of Nazareth acted with insensitivity to his family but with sensitivity to the converts to Christianity.

This attack on the institution of the family is not an isolated event or teaching. In fact, Jesus Christ frequently taught dishonoring of parents and the institution of the family, in direct opposition to the requirements in the 10 Commandments to honor the parents. For instance, in Gospel of Mattthew 8:18-22, one of his disciples came to Jesus Christ to attend the funeral of his father. In fact, as a son, he had the duty to see to the burial of his dead father. This was seen as fulfilling his obligation to honor his parents in the 10 Commandments. One would expect Jesus Christ to be sympathetic to the Christian who just lost his father. One would expect Jesus Christ to say something like: "I am really sorry to hear the news about your father's death. Of course, you should go to your father's funeral. And of course, you should fulfil your duty as a son to have your father buried." This would have been the sensitive thing to say – at least by the standards of today's American custom. Some today would say that this would have been the "human" thing to say.

But Jesus Christ did not say this. Jesus of Nazareth in Matthew 8:22 flatly and insensitively states that it is more important to follow him. And Jesus of Nazareth rudely and sarcastically adds that the dead should bury the dead. Many Americans would call Jesus Christ a jerk for saying something so insensitive. How would you like it if some told you – after you told him that your father just died and that you were headed to his funeral – that your dead father should burry himself and you should not go to his funeral? How would you have felt? What would you say to this guy? Put yourself in the situation of the man in Matthew 8:18-22, and you understand the irreverence of Jesus Christ's statement in a more real way. Jesus Christ deliberately attacked the institution of the family because it was a hindrance for many new converts to Christianity.

Although this rude comment of Jesus Christ would have been a serious insult to the man with the dead father, it would have been a great encouragement for many of his followers gathered to hear his sermons. These new Christians were rejected by their families and many of them disowned. Even if they wanted to go to the funeral of their dead parents, they would not have been able to do so. Jesus Christ's attack of the institution of the family, therefore, was a strategic attempt to encourage Jews to muster the strength to abandon Judaism, which was like abandoning their families.

Early Korean Christians certainly can relate to this. When official government persecutions took place and Christians killed, some of them were ratted out by their own family members and even their parents who held grudge against them for abandoning the ancestral family religion. Many early Korean Christians were disowned by their families and friends for abandoning Buddhism and becoming followers of Jesus Christ. Many early Christians who were rejected by their families for becoming Christians were not allowed to attend the funeral of their parents. The duty, the right, and the honor of burying their dead parents were passed onto others in the family. Many early Korean Christians found comfort in the teaching of Jesus Christ in Matthew 8:18-22. Koreans were not alone in this. In almost every land where Christianity entered, first Christians in that country and even Christians throughout many generations after that had to deal with rejection by their families and being deprived of the right to attend the funeral of their dead parents. History of Christianity holds many records in this regard for thousands of years.

For Christianity, the greatest value is becoming a Christian. In the context of early Christianity, this meant that converts to Christianity would lose their families because their families would have resented their abandonment of the ancestral family religion. Jesus Christ was, in fact, quite extremist in his attack of the institution of the family. In Mark 13:12-14, Jesus Christ states that Christians should expect to be betrayed by their brothers. They should expect to be betrayed by their own father. Children will betray their Christian father and have him put to death for being a Christian. Jesus Christ actively taught that being a Christian means possibly being betrayed to death by one's own family members.

The extremism of Jesus Christ's anti-family teaching is reiterated in Gospel of Luke 12:51-53. This reiterates the teaching of Jesus of Nazareth that he had not come to bring peace to the family but division. He taught that because of him, family members will hate each other. Because of Jesus Christ, father will hate his child and the child will hate the father. Because of Jesus Christ, mother will hate her daughter, and the daughter will hate the mother who gave her birth. Daughter will hate the mother-in-law and vice versa. Jesus Christ taught that this is normal for the followers of Jesus Christ. This is an extreme teaching and is very anti-family and certainly disrespects the 10 Commandments. But as extreme as it sounds, in the historical context of Jesus Christ's ministry, this was a normal occurrence for many converts to Christianity. If a son converted to Christianity and abandoned Judaism, the father would hate him and disown him. This still goes on many orthodox Jewish families around the world. If a daughter abandoned the family ancestral religion and refused to marry a nice religious Jewish boy down the street, the mother would take personal offense and hate the daughter. This was actually happening at Jesus Christ's time with those who converted to Christianity and followed Jesus Christ. The same was the case with the daughter-in-law who converted to Christianity. As the result of her conversion, the daughter-in-law abandoned many traditional Jewish practices tied to the Jewish religion. This would have angered her mother-in-law and brought down her hatred.

The extremist anti-family position of Jesus Christ is encapsulated in his proclamation in Luke 14:26. Jesus Christ proclaims: "If anyone comes to me and does not hate his father and mother, his wife and children, his brothers and sisters – yes, even his own life – he cannot be my disciple." Most scholars, even the most critical scholars, agree that this is an authentic saying of Jesus of Nazareth.

It was a part of Jesus Christ's core teaching to break the 10 Commands and dishonor the parents for the sake of Jesus Christ. The fact that Jesus Christ taught hating of one's parents raised the concern of many community members who were interested in seeing peace and order in their communities. For many, Jesus Christ was the greatest trouble-maker they met. How dare he teach people to hate their parents? But Jesus Christ did and in many places.

Again, the historical context of the ministry of Jesus of Nazareth should be appreciated. Jews who followed Jesus Christ were abandoning Judaism, which was the ancestral religion. There were reactions to this. Many family members perceived this as a rejection of the family itself. The Jewish father took it personally that his son abandoned Judaism and often disowned him for it. There were many among Jesus Christ's followers who were intensely hated by their own family members. In this light, the message to hate one's family would have come as a relief and encouragement. But this does not lessen the impact or the nature of Jesus Christ's teaching. It is a fact of history that Jesus taught his disciples to dishonor their parents and hate them if it meant following Jesus Christ.

It was such teaching that allowed Christianity to spread wide and far. Judaism which emphasizes honoring of parents as a fundamental religious value could not win many converts because the teaching itself presents people of other religions from dishonoring or alienating their parents by converting to Judaism. In Judaism, honoring of parents is a fundamental value or the highest value. In contrast, Christian texts do not encourage honoring of parents. Certainly, the Gospels and the teachings of Jesus Christ is the best proof of this. Christianity emphasizes abandoning family and even hating the family if it means following Jesus Christ. It is because this is the most important value in Christianity that Christianity spread across cultures and different religion areas. Christianity has a fundamental mechanism built inside the system of Christianity that allows the converts to abandon their ancestral religion and even their own family for the sake of Jesus Christ. That is why Christianity is the most wide-spread religion across cultures and geographical boundaries.

Whether Jesus Christ intended this to be the fundamental core of Christianity for generations and generations or if Jesus of Nazareth was merely reacting to the events and realities of his time is debated among many academics. But it is a fact of history that the New Testament became the canon of the Christian religion that prioritizes the teaching of Jesus Christ as a normative rule for the followers of the religion across time and space. And it had the historical effect of helping many people to abandon their ancestral religions and even their families to become Christians. And it is a historical fact that Jesus of Nazareth actually taught hating of one's family, whatever his motivations may have been. It is a fundamental part of historic Christianity that followers of Jesus Christ must hate their parents if it means following Jesus Christ.

One can see that subversion was a fundamental part of the Christian faith from the very beginning. Jesus Christ subverted Judaism and the Mosaic Law in an effort to win followers. And followers of Jesus Christ continued this tradition. The key signifier of "up to half the kingdom" represents a consistent policy among early Christians to subvert Judaism and win converts to Christianity.

The key signifier of "up to half the kingdom" can be called a negative key signifier or subversive key signifier because it inverts or subverts the key signifier already in place within Judaism of Jesus Christ's time. This key signifier in the Bible is very important to the general discussion of key signifiers as a literary device because it shows both the positive use of the key signifier and the negative or subversive use of the key signifier in Biblical literature. There are many key signifiers in the Bible, and it is my hope that this book defining and explaining the nature and function of the key signifier as a literary device will encourage many other scholars to investigate and contribute to the study of key signifiers in the Bible. There is a wealth of key signifiers in the Bible, and this chapter represents

68

only the tip of the iceberg. There is no doubt that scholars seeking to investigate key signifiers in the Bible will be rewarded in wonderful ways.

Chapter 3

The Apocrypha and the Pseudepigrapha

In chapter 2, we have seen how the key signifier functions as a literary device in the Bible. In this chapter, we will investigate how the key signifier functions in a body of literature that has come to be known as the Apocrypha and the Pseudepigrapha. By this category, scholars generally refer to literary works that were composed in the intertestamental period, or the period between the completion of the last book in the Old Testament and the composition of the first book of the New Testament. Of course, this is only a general description of what we call the Apocrypha and the Pseudepigrapha. Academics are still debating what precisely belongs to this body of literature.

To give a picture of the complexities of the field, the question still lingers whether the Dead Sea Scrolls should be included in the academic category of the Apocrypha and the Pseudepigrapha. The Dead Sea Scrolls are a body of literature that was discovered when a Bedouin threw a rock into a cave in Qumran in the Judean Desert in the land of Palestine. He was searching for his lost animal. But the rock broke a jar in the cave, and thus a whole body of literature was discovered. No one was aware of the existence of this body of literature before the discovery by the Bedouin. Since the scrolls dated to the time of the intertestamental period, the excitement in the academic community was immense. Much of the 20th century can be seen as fixated on the Dead Sea Scrolls. There were scholars entrusted with production of critical editions of the scrolls. When the critical editions were slow in coming, many academics wanting to use them for research into the study of ancient Jewish history and for examination of intertestamental literature became agitated. Now, most of the findings have been published.

In the 20th century, the study of Dead Sea Scrolls had so seriously impacted the field of Biblical studies that other areas took a beating. One such area was the study of the Apocrypha and the Pseudepigrapha. As Dead Sea Scrolls research gained ascendancy and dominance quickly, it became a field in its own. No one seriously questioned the relationship of the Dead Sea Scrolls to the body of literature known as the Apocrypha and the Pseudepigrapha, which in fact had dominated the study of the intertestamental period for two thousand years.

This reality is best encapsulated in the founding of a major research center to tackle the study of intertestamental period literature at the Hebrew University of Jerusalem in the academic year 1995-96. Professor Michael Stone, who is a renown expert in the field of the Apocrypha and the Pseudepigrapha, founded an institute at the Hebrew University of Jerusalem to investigate his field of expertise. He, too, had caught the Dead Sea Scrolls research fever. Despite the fact that his main field of expertise was the Apocrypha and the Pseudepigrapha, he named his new academic center "Orion Center for the Study of the Dead Sea Scrolls and Associated Literature." There was not even a mention of the Apocrypha or the Pseudepigrapha. They were relegated to the background and to the periphery in the attachment "Associated Literature." I was one of the two interns during the founding year of 1995-96 (the other one was Martina van den Berg from Utrecht University in Holland). I asked Michael this question, but he just fudged an answer. I guess the question never even entered his mind. But Professor Stone was not alone in catching the Dead Sea Scrolls fever. Many centers of Dead Sea Scrolls research cropped up around the world and most of them ignored the study of the Apocrypha and the Pseudepigrapha.

Despite the fact that the study of the Apocrypha and the Pseudepigrapha has taken a back seat to the study of Dead Sea Scroll literature, it is an undeniable fact of history that they have been crucial for understanding the intertestamenal period for two thousand years. Even now, the framework for investigating the period is built on centuries of investigation into the Apocrypha and the Pseudepigrapha. It would be fair to say, despite vast amounts of research on the Dead Sea Scrolls, it has not changed the fundamental framework built in the past before the discovery of the Dead Sea Scrolls. And in a way, it would be legitimate to say that Dead Sea Scrolls should fit under the category of the Apocrypha and the Pseudepigrapha. But elation for Dead Sea Scroll research is still high and most academics do not think to question the categories formed as the result of the initial excitement over the study of the Dead Sea Scrolls.

To add to the complexity of the field known as the Apocrypha and the Pseudepigrapha, we can look at what has come to be known as "New Testament Apocrypha." New Testament Apocrypha are works written after the earthly ministry of Jesus Christ about him or the early Christian apostles with the flavor of the New Testament. They were composed at the contemporaneous time as the composition of the New Testament. But New Testament Apocrypha books were not included in the Bible. For example, the Gospel of Thomas belongs in this category of New Testament Apocrypha. The Gospel of Thomas is a Gnostic text that denigrates the human side of Jesus Christ and the material world. It is supposedly an account of the life of Jesus Christ like other Gospels included in the Christian canon. Because the Gospel of Thomas is not a part of the Christian canon, it is not referred to as a New Testament book. Thus, it has been relegated to the position of being a New Testament Apocrypha. For a good sampling of New Testament Apocrypha, you can take a look at the book edited by Wilhelm Schneemelcher, entitled *New Testament Apocrypha*. Currently, there is no academic consensus whether this body of literature should be a category on its own or it should belong to the category known as the Apocrypha and the Pseudepigrapha.

Generally and functionally, the body of literature that is referred to as the Apocrypha and the Pseudepigrapha in the academic community is literature that was included in the edited book by R. H. Charles, entitled *The Apocrypha and Pseudepigrapha of the Old Testament in English*, published in 1913. In a sense, it would not be wrong to say that this book was instrumental in defining the field as such. A more recent key player in the definition of the field is Professor James H. Charlesworth of Princeton Theological Seminary. His representative work in this regard is in a two volume book edited by him, entitled *The Old Testament Pseudepigrapha*. By in large, Charlesworth follows the framework presented in the 1913 work by Charles.

For the purposes of this book, it is not necessary to define precisely what the field of the Apocrapha and the Psuedepigrapha is. As long as we understand what can potentially belong to this category and what is generally recognized to be belonging to this category, that is sufficient enough. Like Biblical literature, the Apocrypha and the Pseudepigrapha have important key signifiers that open up the semantic and experiential fields relating to the collective memory and community value present at the time of the composition of the texts.

As with the investigation of the Bible in chapter 2, we will approach the reality of the key signifier as an important literary device in the Apocrypha and the Pseudepigrapha through a specific example in a representative text. That text will be Psalms of Solomon 11.

Psalms of Solomon, chapter 11, is a part of the Psalms of Solomon, which is a coherent book of poetry with 18 chapters. It is similar to the Biblical book of Psalms in that the structure is heavily poetic. Even in terms of theme and expressions, there are a lot of psalmic materials. But there are some key differences between the Biblical book of Psalms and the Pseudepigrapha book of the Psalms of Solomon. Whereas the former is self-contained in each chapter – that is, each chapter stands alone – the Psalms of Solomon seems to be a type of coherent narrative, albeit a poetic one. In other words, the flow of the Biblical book of Psalms does not tell a coherent story; each chapter stands alone. In fact, when we look at the flow of the chapters in Psalms, they are disjunctive. In a way, we can describe the Biblical book of Psalms as being like a pearl necklace – each pearl is a self-contained unit and these pearls are strung together to make a beautiful necklace.

In contrast, the Pseudepigrapha book of the Psalms of Solomon is more like a narrative story. It is possible to take each chapter apart, and they will be able to stand alone as a self-contained unit. But each chapter is not meant to stand alone. The previous chapter enlightens and anticipates the following chapter, and the following chapter satisfies the suspense created by the previous chapter. In this sense, the Psalms of Solomon shares some similarities with Homer's *Odyssey* or *Iliad*. But the Psalms of Solomon is not as coherent and cannot be seen quite as the narrative in the same sense.

The academic consensus is that this work is from the first century B.C. In particular, Psalms of Solomon, chapter 2, is often pointed out as the decisive evidence of this. There are some resemblances with the life of Pompeii. Psalms of Solomon 2 describes a man, described as a "sinner" who was a military conqueror, who invaded Jerusalem. And this man died in Egypt. The scholarly consensus at the moment is that this is a description of Pompeii. Based on this consensus and argument, the Pseudepigrapha book of the Psalms of Solomon is dated toward the end of the 1st century BC, within a few decades of the birth of Jesus of Nazareth. There is a minority scholarly position that the work dates from the time of the Maccabees and describes the events relating to the Hasmonean dynasty. This minority position dates the Psalms of Solomon to the 2nd century B.C. There are textual proofs scattered throughout the Psalms of Solomon, which warrant further investigation of this minority position. In the past, it has had the greatest support among German scholars.

The content of Psalms of Solomon can be summarized in this way. There are descriptions of sins committed by Jews. These sins bring about the judgement

74

of God according to the poet who wrote the Psalms of Solomon. The judgement was in the form of Gentile nations invading and conquering Jerusalem and defiling the Jerusalem Temple. The poet of the Psalms of Solomon beseeches his readers toward pure worship of God and to keep the covenant made with God. Although the poet describes Jews as violators of the covenant who rightly deserve the punishment they received, he is careful to exonerate God from all liability. He describes God as righteous and faithful in judging Israel for its sins. In fact, the poet seems to fault God on the side of being too merciful toward covenant breakers. The poet expresses his hope in the deliverance of God. Last two chapters of the Psalms of Solomon – namely, chapters 17 and 18 – are often seen as messianic in nature. Professor William Horbury of Cambridge University characterizes this messiah as a transcendent Davidic messiah to be raised up by God at the appointed time.[5]

Psalms of Solomon 11 is nearly at the half point of the work. In it, the poet composer expresses his hope that God will deliver Jerusalem. In fact, Psalms of Solomon 11 is one of the most coherent psalms (or chapter) out of the 18 psalms (chapters). Here is my rendition of Psalms of Solomon 11:

Blow the trumpet in Zion to gather the holy ones!
Proclaim in Jerusalem the voice of him who brings good news
Because God is visiting Israel in pity.
Jerusalem, stand up high and see your children
Being gathered by the Lord from the East and the West.
They come from the North rejoicing in their God
And God has gathered them from far off islands.
He levelled high mountains for them
And the hills fled when they entered.
Woods provided them with shelter as they passed by

[5] William Horbury, *Messianism among Jews and Christians: Twelve Biblical and Historical Studies* (London: T. & T. Clark, 2003), p. 62.

And God caused sweet smelling tree to spring up for them
So that Israel could pass by with the presence of the glory of their God.
Jerusalem, put on your beautiful clothing!
And prepare your holy priestly robe
Because God has proclaimed good regarding Israel, forever.
May the Lord carry out his words regarding Israel and Jerusalem!
May the Lord lift up Jerusalem by his glorious name!
May the Mercy of the Lord be upon Israel forever!

As we can see, Psalms of Solomon 11 is a beautiful poem that coheres nicely. There is a beginning, a middle, and a conclusion. Scholars have struggled to find a historical place to put this psalm, however. If, indeed, the scholarly consensus is true and the poem belongs to the 1st century BC, how could we explain the content of this poem? There does not seem to be any historical reality purported by this poem. There was not a massive ingathering of Jews from the East, West, North, and far off islands.

In fact, the historical movement was in the other direction. In the first century BC, we find the Jews scattering throughout the Roman Empire. In fact, Alexandria in Egypt was becoming a major center for the Jews and many educated Jews preferred Alexandria to Egypt. It is no accident that the greatest Jewish philosopher from Late Antiquity came from Alexandria, Egypt. Of course, we are talking about Philo of Alexandria. In first century BC, the Jewish community in Alexandria was growing and growing.

Alexandria was not the only place outside of Israel where Jews were moving to. Jews were scattering everywhere. Some Jews departed Israel and the Jerusalem Temple for religious reasons. In fact, when the Hasmoneans took over the position of the high priest of the Jerusalem Temple, typically reserved for Zadokite priests, the legitimate priestly line of Zadok, departed *en masse* and set up a rival Jewish temple in Leontopolis, Egypt. When you have priests of

Jerusalem Temple leaving Israel for Egypt, it is understandable that many Jews who were not of the priestly class felt justified in departing Jerusalem and Israel for Gentile lands. And this is precisely what happened.

Beside Zadokite priests who left Jerusalem to build a rival Jewish Temple in Egypt, there were other religious Jews who departed Jerusalem to set up a Jewish religious community elsewhere. A major sect of Jews who did this was the Essenes. The most famous Essene community is found in Qumran. They are the Jewish sect that produced the Dead Sea Scrolls, discussed earlier. *The Hodayot Scrolls* (1QH) describes the conflict between the Teacher of Righteousness, who is thought to be the founder of the Qumran community, and the "Wicked Priest" of the Jerusalem Temple. Based on this and the fact that Qumranites often referred to themselves as sons of Zadok, it is understood that the Qumran community represents another strand of Zadokite priests who fled Jerusalem when the Hasmoneans took power in the Jerusalem Temple. Their life as those belonging to the legitimate priestly line was in jeopardy because the Hasmoneans not only took over the Jerusalem Temple but also usurped the political rule of Jerusalem, making themselves, in effect, royal rulers of Jerusalem.

Whereas the Zadokites who went off to Egypt and set a rival Jewish temple in Leontopolis seemingly abandoned their hope of presiding in the Jerusalem Temple, the Zadokites who ran off to the desert in Qumran seemed to harbor hopes of return to the Jerusalem Temple. *The Temple Scroll* (11QT) is a testimony to this aspiration. Qumranites hoped for an eschatological redemption and considered themselves the righteous remnant who found favor with God. They believed that all the priests of the Jerusalem Temple, whom they considered unrighteous usurpers of the Jerusalem Temple, would be killed in the eschatological judgement by God's divine punishment, paving the way for their priestly service in the Jerusalem Temple. Strong invective along these lines is found in *Pesher Habbakuk* (1QpHab).

Although Qumran community members perceived their future in the Jerusalem Temple, instituting what they perceived was correct worship there at the eschatological time, not all the members of the Qumran community were priests. In fact, those who were not of the priestly families could join the Qumran community. Regulations regarding joining the Qumran sect are outlined in *The Community Rule* (1QS). Qumran community was a strict, monastic community, which discouraged male members from engaging in sexual relations. The jury is still out in terms of explaining the diachronic development of communal ideology – such as radical sexual asceticism which seems incompatible with normative Jewish rules for Jewish priest and non-priests alike. But it is often assumed that the Qumran community became more and more radical as time passed, and generation after generation did not see a restoration to the Jerusalem Temple, which they hoped for.

Both the Zadokite temple in Leontopolis and the Zadokite led community in Qumran illustrate that there was scattering away from Jerusalem, rather than ingathering into Jerusalem. These two communities were founded in the 2nd century BC, but were thought to be running in the 1st century BC as well. In fact, last two century before the birth of Jesus of Nazareth represented a tremendous movement of Jews away from Jerusalem and Diaspora areas. Jews are thought to have gone as far as Rome and Spain, where Jewish communities were thought to have been created and maintained.

Given this reality, how can we explain Psalms of Solomon 11? Obviously, it is not a poem describing a historical reality. We can understand Psalms of Solomon as describing a situation after the Exile when the Jews were gathered back in Jerusalem. But there is a deliberate attempt not to identify the poem specifically with this return. Miraculous ingathering elevates the poem to the mythic realms, giving it an eschatological, supernatural character. I would argue that this was deliberate so that the poem could represent any kind of ingathering/return to Jerusalem. It could be read as a poem representing the ingathering of the Exiles back to Jerusalem. It could be read as representing the Exodus into Jerusalem. It could even be read in an unspecified future time to refer to an ingathering that is to come after some kind of displacement and scattering of Jews away from Jerusalem.

In this regard, I would argue that this poem is liturgical in nature. Psalms of Solomon was composed with an intention to be recited by the Jewish community as a liturgy in personal piety or religious worship. Like the Biblical book of Psalms, Psalms of Solomon 11 could be read in communal worship settings as liturgy or used in individual prayers in personal liturgy.

Now, that we have described the nature of Psalms of Solomon 11 in some length and are aware of the historical context and the content of the poem, we can tackle the central issue related with this book – namely, the key signifier in Psalms of Solomon 11. The key signifier in Psalms of Solomon 11 is "forever."

"Forever" is found twice in Psalms of Solomon 11. For the purpose of facilitating analysis, I will present the two lines with the word in it, here. First, we have: "Because God has proclaimed good regarding Israel, forever." And second, we have: "May the Mercy of the Lord be upon Israel forever!" The second attestation of "forever" is found, in fact, in the final line of the poem, embodied in Psalms of Solomon 11.

We notice that both attestations of "forever" are found in the context of God showing favor to Israel. The first attestation recalls the proclamation of God that is positively inclined toward Israel. The second attestation is a wishful thinking that God will keep his proclamation. And it is in this note of wishful thinking that Psalms of Solomon 11 ends.

As we recall, for a word or phrase to be a key signifier, it has to have a double layered trigger mechanism. It has to trigger collective memory or community value that is tied to semantic and experiential world of the past (or present), on the one hand. On the other hand, the key signifier also has to trigger the audience – either readers or listeners – to some kind of concrete action. In light of this, let us begin to answer the question of how "forever" is a key signifier in Psalms of Solomon 11.

We will first discuss the first part of the dual layered trigger mechanism – namely, the triggering of collective memory and community value. Which collective memory and community value does the key signifier of "forever" trigger? I would argue that the central collective memory being triggered is the Abrahamic covenant found in the book of Genesis.

The covenant of God with Abraham, found in the book of Genesis, is the central covenant in the Old Testament. Theologians have talked about the Noahic covenant as a covenant that precedes the Abrahamic covenant, but the problem is that it does not play any serious role in the context of the rest of the Old Testament. In other words, Noahic covenant is localized in the narrative about Noah. What was the Noahic covenant? It is generally referred to as the promise of God that he would never destroy the whole world by a single flood.

Some theologians – particularly, Reformed Christian theologians – like to talk about the Adamic covenant. But again, this covenant does not play a serious role in the Old Testament. In fact, when Christian theologians talk about the Adamic covenant, they almost always mention Jesus Christ as the Second Adam or the Last Adam. They often talk about sin entering the world through the First Adam – that is, the Adam of the book of Genesis. Salvation, they argue, entered through the Last Adam – that is, Jesus Christ. As we can see, Adamic covenant can be quite important in Christian theology, which centralizes the work of salvation by Jesus Christ. But it really has no impact on Jewish thought. Certainly, it did not play a major role in the Old Testament.

Thus, it would not be wrong to talk about the Abrahamic covenant as not only the most important covenant in the Bible, but the foundational covenant in the Old Testament. In fact, when the Old Testament mentions the word covenant without any qualifiers, it is assumed that it is referring to the Abrahamic covenant.

Even the covenant made in Mount Sinai through Moses is seen as an extension or a type of fulfilment of the Abrahamic covenant.

Because the Abrahamic covenant was the most important covenant in the Old Testament, it was firmly imbedded in the collective memory of Jews from the earliest times. And the Abrahamic covenant crops up again and again throughout Old Testament literature, thereby reinforcing the collective memory built directly on the Abrahamic covenant. Thus, it is easy to see how "forever" functioned as an important key signifier in Late Second Temple Judaism.

Let us examine in more specific detail how the key signifier of "forever" recalls the collective memory of the Abrahamic covenant. The place to start is with the actual text that describes the making of the Abrahamic covenant. There are two Biblical texts that describe the covenant that God made with Abraham – namely, Genesis 15 and Genesis 17. Critical scholars often assume that there was only one covenant made and that these two chapters describe the same event, but in different ways. This would be similar to two creation accounts in the book of Genesis – namely, Genesis 1:1-2:3 and Genesis 2:4-25. Both creation accounts are seen as describing the same event, but in different ways.

Out of the two chapters in Genesis describing the covenant made between God and Abraham, Genesis 17 is a more developed text. And most Old Testament texts referring to the covenant between God and Abraham refer to Genesis 17 and not to Genesis 15. This is clear from the content. This is the case with extra-biblical materials referring to the Abrahamic covenant as well. And this is certainly the case with the Psalms of Solomon.

When we look at Genesis 17, we see that it has the word "forever" (or "everlasting") in it. In Hebrew, "forever" or "everlasting" is *olam* (or *le-olam*). The Abrahamic covenant in Genesis 17 uses this word as a central element in the covenant made with Abraham. "Forever" (or "everlasting") is such an important part of the Abrahamic covenant that I argue that it is a kind of a kind of covenant seal or a signature signing the covenant.

Let us examine the attestation of "forever" (or "everlasting") in Genesis 17. The word *olam*, or "forever"/"everlasting," is found four times in Genesis 17 – namely, in verses 7, 8, 13, 19. We will examine each of the occurrence to see the significance of its function in its context.

Genesis 17:7 states that God is establishing an "everlasting" (or "forever") covenant with Abraham and his descendants for generations to come to be his God and the God of his descendants after him. In a sense, "everlasting"/"forever" (Hebrew word *olam*) seals this stipulation of the covenant. God's obligation is to be the God of Abraham and Abraham's descendants. And this is an obligation "forever."

The second attestation of *olam* is found in Genesis 17:8. Here, again, covenantal obligation that God is to fulfil is outlined. Genesis 17:8 states that God will give the whole land of Canaan, where Abraham was a foreigner, as the possession of Abraham and his descendants "forever." In other words, God's part in the covenant was to give the ownership of the land of Canaan to Abraham and Abraham's descendants, forever. Again, "forever"/"everlasting" seals the stipulation of the covenant. In the case of Genesis 17:8, the stipulation referred to God's obligations in the covenant.

But God's obligations, as outlined in Genesis 17:7 and Genesis 17:8, is dependent on the actions of the other covenanting party, namely Abraham (and his descendants). God does not need to fulfil his "everlasting" covenant if Abraham or his descendants do not fulfil their requirements in the covenant. This is clear in Genesis 17:9-13. It states that Abraham and his descendants must keep their part of the covenant.

What is the covenantal requirement for Abraham and his descendants? They must circumcise every male member. The males who are to be circumcised include Abraham, every male descendants of Abraham (to be circumcised on the eighth day), and every male slave or servant including Gentiles. In modern day terms, not only Jewish boys born to Jewish parents are to be circumcised, but everybody on the payroll of Jewish individuals are to be forced circumcision according to the Jewish religious mandate. It is not difficult to see how difficult it would be to satisfy this stipulation placed on Abraham and his descendants. The difficulty is illustrated in the fact that it would be like requiring every Palestinian paid to do work for the State of Israel – for instance, as a janitor in a state hospital – having to go a circumcision. This would apply to Filipino and Hungarian temporary workers employed in state of Israel's road building project having to undergo circumcision. Abraham and his descendants were to circumcise all who are employed by them. Failure to have them circumcised would constitute failure to observe their stipulation of the covenant. Thus, they would have broken their part in the Abrahamic covenant, and God would be released from having to fulfil his part of the Abrahamic covenant.

In fact, the requirement of Abraham and Abraham's descendants to circumcise their descendants and their foreign employees is described as an "everlasting"/"forever" requirement in Genesis 17:13. The Genesis 17:13 attestation represents the third attestation of "forever" – which is *olam* in Hebrew. Genesis 17:14 indicates that even one males not being circumcised who is required to be circumcised constitutes breaking of the covenant by Abraham and his descendants. This would obviously release God from his covenantal obligations.

The fourth and final attestation of "forever"/"everlasting" is found in Genesis 17:19. This attestation is not as significant as the first three attestations. First three attestations actually signed the covenant and indicated the forever nature of the stipulations of the covenant by both parties. Breaking of the stipulations by one party would release the other party from the requirement to observe the covenant. In the case of the fourth attestation, "forever" is more descriptive in nature. Genesis 17:19 describing Sarah, Abraham's wife having a son, and the covenant that is to be forever would continue through him as well. Although descriptive, the fact that "forever" (*olam*) is used here as well underscores the emphasis that the term is an essential part of the covenant and this essential character of the covenant in a sense encapsulates the nature of the covenant. It is not surprising, therefore, that "forever" came to be integrally associated with the semantic and experiential reference to the collective memory of the Abrahamic covenant.

Likewise, "forever" functions as a key signifier in Psalms of Solomon 11. The two occurrences of forever immediately open up the semantic and experiential reference to the collective memory of the Abrahamic covenant. In other words, the key signifier of "forever" triggers the collective memory of the Abrahamic covenant and its requirements.

In this context, we understand what Psalms of Solomon 11 is essentially referring to. Let us remind ourselves the two attestations of forever in Psalms of Solomon 11. The first attestation is: "Because God has proclaimed good regarding Israel, forever." And the second attestation is: "May the Mercy of the Lord be upon Israel forever!"

In light of our discussion of the Abrahamic covenant in Genesis 17, we can understand the first attestation of the key signifier of "forever" in Psalms of Solomon 11 to be referring to God's obligations to the Abrahamc covenant found in Genesis 17:7 and Genesis 17:8. God's first obligation to the Abraham's covenant (Genesis 17:7) was that he would be the God of Abraham and Abraham's descendants, forever. God's second obligation to the covenant was that he would give the ownership of the land of Canaan to Abraham and his descendants forever. In this regard, the line in Psalms of Solomon containing the first key signifier of "forever" makes sense – "Because God has proclaimed good regarding Israel, forever."

Whereas the first attestation of the key signifier of "forever" in Psalms of Solomon 11 recalls the collective memory of the obligations of God to the Abrahamic covenant, the second attestation of the key signifier of "forever" in Psalms of Solomon 11 recalls the collective memory of the obligations of

Abraham and his descendants to the Abrahamic covenant. As we recall from Genesis 17:13 and its preceding verses that are integrally related to it, the requirement of Abraham and his descendants to the covenant is for them to circumcise every male born into the household of Abraham's descendants as well as every slave or servant employed by Jews.

The poet of Psalms of Solomon 11 knew that the covenantal obligations for Abraham and his descendants were not being met. The poet knew that because the Jews were breaking their obligations to the covenant, God was right not to keep his part of the Abrahamic covenant. God could abandon the Jewish people and no longer be their God. And God could give away the ownership of the land of Canaan to Gentiles. It would be God's right to do this in light of the fact that Jews broke their stipulation of the Abrahamic covenant, which they were to keep forever. This is why the poet beseeches God's mercy. As we recall the second attestation of the key signifier of "forever" is found in this sentence: "May the Mercy of the Lord be upon Israel forever!"

Indeed, there is no doubt in the poet's mind that the requirement for Abraham and his descendants to the Abrahamic covenant was not being met. It is not surprising to see how this stipulation was being broken when we look at Jewish history of the period. The last two centuries before the birth of Jesus of Nazareth was a period marked by rampant Hellenism in Palestine. It was not only those who were not religious who were influenced by Hellenism. In fact, the whole Israeli society was thoroughly impacted by Hellenism. The impact of Hellenism was so profound and pervasive that even the high priest of the Jerusalem Temple was thoroughly Hellenized.

The period leading up to the Maccabean Revolt in the 2nd century B.C. was marked by various priestly factions trying to court favor from Hellenistic rulers. The two great Hellenistic powers were Egypt and Syria. There was a pro-Egyptian faction and a pro-Syrian faction. Members of each faction supported and appealed to their respective Hellenistic ruler for favor and influence.

Whether the Egyptian or the Syrian faction won out, the result was the same. It was a process of Hellenization by the Jerusalem Temple leadership not only of Jewish worship but also of cultural practices of the Jewish people in Palestine.

Although the Maccabean Revolt was seen as an act of Jewish religious renewal and return to traditional Judaism, the religious zeal was short lived in Jerusalem. Jerusalem Temple worship under the Hasmoneans – those who had led the Maccabean Revolt and succeeded – were just as eager as their predecessors to aid in the process of Hellenization of the Jewish population as time passed.

In fact, the Hasmoneans angered many traditionalists by usurping the power of the monarchy. Instead of placing a person from the Davidic line on the throne of Jerusalem, Hasmonean priests became kings and combined the institution of the Jerusalem Temple and the institution of the monarchy. Their disrespect for traditional separation of powers reflected their disrespect for traditional Jewish ways in terms of religious observance and worship.

It was during the period of the Hasmoneans that Hellenism pervaded throughout Jerusalem. There were not only Jews not getting circumcised, there were those who tried to cover up their circumcision through an operation. They were ashamed of their circumcision as they competed in Hellenistic games and sport, which was often done in the nude. Thus, the direct command to be circumcised was being violated by Hellenized Jewish masses, and the Jerusalem Temple leadership and Hellenized religious leaders were a central part of the problem.

But the Jews were not only violating the letter of the law; they were violating the spirit of the law. The Abraham covenant required circumcision as the letter of the law from Abraham and his descendants, but this came to be understood to reach into the spirit of the law, which was cultic observation. The covenant between Abraham and God was made when there was no Jerusalem Temple or laws regarding Temple sacrifice and worship based on the Jerusalem

Temple. In fact, the covenant between God and Abraham was made even before the existence of the Tabernacle, which was seen as a precursor to the Jerusalem Temple. The birth of Moses was several centuries away.

The time of the Abrahamic covenant, according to the Genesis narrative, represented a period when there was not a people of Israel, yet. It was Abraham's grandson, Jacob, who came to be called Israel. It was Jacob's twelve sons who represented the twelve tribes of Israel that was to come into existence. Abraham only had his family with him in Canaan. He was a foreigner there. Abraham was not even of the same race as the people who lived in Canaan. Abraham's origins lay in modern day Iran and Iraq.

Since none of Israel's religious institutions, including the Mosaic Law, existed at the time of the Abrahamic covenant, those elements could not have been included in the covenant stipulations. Circumcision, in a sense, was the first cultic requirement. But in the letter of the law, the spirit of the law was required. Just as Abraham and his descendants were to keep the cultic obligation of circumcision, which was the letter of the law, they were to keep the spirit of the law, which came to be cultic obligations to the Jerusalem Temple. This reality is clearly evident in Deuteronomy 29, which can be seen as an updated explanation of the covenant in the context of a time when Israel existed as a people and were required cultic worship. In this sense, Deuteronomy 29 can be seen as *gemara*, or commentary, on the covenant made with Abraham.

When we look at Deuteronomy 29, this becomes clear. Deuteronomy 29:12-15 explicitly reminds the Israelites at the time of Moses about the Abrahamic covenant. Furthermore, it explains the principle that the covenant made with the people present is binding on those who are not physically present in the covenant making/renewal ceremony but those who are included as the party making the covenant with God. As we recall from the Abrahamic covenant, the party making the covenant with God was Abraham and his descendants, who were not present or even born at the time of the covenant making between God and Abraham. This commentary, or *gemara*, explains the forever nature of the covenant stipulations. And Deuteronomy 29:12-15 reiterates God's obligations to the Abrahamic covenant that he is to be the God of Abraham and his descendants.

It is interesting to note that Deuteronomy 29:12-15 is missing the word "forever." But this makes sense in the context of Deuteronomy. The covenant renewal ceremony followed exodus from Egypt. Jews were slaves in Egypt for hundreds of years. Clearly, this shows that God had violated his second obligation to the Abrahamic covenant, which was that he would give the land of Canaan as the property of Abraham and his descendants forever. Obviously, Canaan did not belong to the descendants of Abraham. They had just barely escaped the grips of the Egyptian Pharaoh after centuries of servitude in Egypt. To many Israeli minds, this also meant that God ceased to be their God in Egypt. What happened to the promise that God would be the God of Abraham and Abraham's descendants forever?

It was because of questions like this that the Deuteronomy 29 was presented as a commentary, or *gemara*, on the Abrahamic covenant. It explains why God violated his obligations to the Abrahamic covenant. It was because Israelis first violated their requirements to the Abrahamic covenant. This explanation is clear in Deuteronomy 29:24-28. This commentary explains that God will bring down the curses of the covenant if Israelis worship other gods, which is shown to be a covenant violation. Circumcision was the letter of the law, but cultic observance in properly worshiping God was the spirit of the law. Following other gods or sacrificing to idols, in effect, violated the spirit of the cultic requirement for Abraham and his descendants.

In fact, one of the two accounts of the Abrahamic covenant anticipates God's violation of his obligations to the Abrahamic covenant. If we recall, the Abrahamic covenant is accounted in Genesis 15 and Genesis 17. Genesis 15 is the shorter, less developed version and Genesis 17 is the more developed, longer version. In Genesis 15:13, we see that descendants of Abraham will be enslaved for four hundred years outside of Canaan. Genesis 15 anticipates Israelis breaking their covenantal requirement and God punishing them for it. Like Deuteronomy 29, Genesis 15 does not have the word "forever." We realize from Deuteronomy 29 that the "forever" of God's blessings is dependent on "forever" observance by the descendants of Abraham.

Functionally, the commentary, or *gemara*, of Deuteronomy 29 has the force of reinforcing the key signifier of "forever" attached to the Abrahamic covenant. It was true that God would be the God of Abraham and his descendants forever. It was true that God would give the land of Canaan as a possession of Abraham and his descendants forever. But this was conditional on the cultic observance of Abraham and his descendants, which was their obligation to the covenant, which was to be a requirement forever.

Deuteronomy 29 is a good example of how "forever" came to be a key signifier in Jewish collective memory. Old Testament literature defined and explained the nature of "forever" in the Abrahamic covenant as found in Genesis 17. What did it mean for God to keep his covenantal obligations forever? What was it conditional upon? When can God violate the "forever" stipulation? What was the obligation of the Jews?

In this light, we can fully understand why Psalms of Solomon ends in a note of hope and supplication to God. "May the Mercy of the Lord be upon Israel forever!" The poet recognized that Jews had violated their covenant obligation to God. He recognized that God had the right to break the covenant and bring down the curses of the covenant. He knew this because Genesis 17 along with Deuteronomy 29 and other Old Testament literature expounding on the Abrahamic covenant became an integral part of Jewish collective memory. Knowing this, the poet expresses his wishful desire that God will show mercy.

We understand now how "forever" triggers the semantic and experiential reference to the collective memory of Jews at the time of the composition of Psalms of Solomon 11. But a key signifier is not a key signifier if it merely triggers collective memory; it must also trigger an action based on the triggering of the collective memory. There must be a dual layered triggering function.

The logical question to ask at this point is: What action does the key signifier of "forever" trigger in Psalms of Solomon 11? I would argue that the key signifier of "forever" will encourage the audience toward proper Temple-centered religious observance. Worshipping God in his temple and not following idols or foreign gods is seen integral to the fulfilment of the covenant with God. Abrahamic covenant filtered through Deuteronomy 29 and Old Testament literature showed that the spirit of the Abrahamic covenant and its obligations for the descendants of Abraham were proper cultic observance associated with the Jerusalem Temple, the dwelling place of the God of Abraham.

The fact that the poet of Psalms of Solomon 11 intended to trigger a proper cultic worship at the Jerusalem Temple through the key signifier of "forever" is further supported by the content of Psalms of Solomon 11 as a whole. The poem describes ingathering of Jews in Jerusalem from the Diaspora for proper cultic worship. The miraculous imagery of mountains being levelled and trees springing up reminds the reader or listener of the miracles that God performed when he delivered Israelites out of Egypt in the Exodus. Why did Moses lead the Israelites out of Egypt against the wishes of the powerful Pharaoh? It was for the reason of properly worshiping God. And by the time of the composition of Psalms of Solomon, proper cultic worship was understood to be required in the Jerusalem Temple.

We are talking about a period which remembered the Exile in Babylon. The Second Temple standing in Jerusalem reminded Jews that they were without the central place of worship for a long time. The Second Temple was a pride for Jews of their deliverance from foreign rule. It is understandable in light of the significance that the Second Temple in Jerusalem received in the collective memory and community value of the Jews in the Late Second Temple period, why the Zedokite temple in Leontopolis failed.

It was true that the Zadokites were the rightful priests to lead the sacrifices and head the cult in the Jerusalem Temple. Hasmoneans were impostors and not rightful priests according to traditional Jewish understanding. But the Exile in Babylon created homesickness and a longing for Jerusalem. Thus, the import of Jerusalem became even more significant in the community value of the Jews in Exile than before the Exile. The Jerusalem Temple became so important that it displaced all other values of traditional Judaism, including the requirement for a Zadokite priest to be the high priest of the Jerusalem Temple. This is why the Jews did not follow the right priests into a temple they constructed in Egypt. By the Late Second Temple period, it was a part of the Jewish community value that proper cultic worship should be done in the Jerusalem Temple. No Jewish temple should be constructed elsewhere. This explains why the Leontopolis Temple became a non-factor very quickly and the Zadokite line there receded into oblivion.

The same was the case with Zadokites in Qumran. It is true that Zadokites are the correct priestly line. And it was probably a good thing to emphasize details of law and religious observance. But such debates were the luxury of scholars and not of the common people. All they knew was that they were in Exile for many years. The Second Temple in Jerusalem represented a restoration, a deliverance from God. Jews in the Second Temple period believed that the very existence of the Jerusalem Temple was a sign that God was with them. They were not going to go off into the desert in a self-imposed Exile when the symbol of God's presence among Jews stood right there in Jerusalem. That is why the Qumran community failed to grow. That is why the record was lost about their existence although discoveries in Qumran in the 20th century revealed that the library in Qumran was among the most extensive in the ancient world insofar as Judaism was concerned. What did the average Joe Israel need with all those debates about finer points of the Jewish religion? The fact was that the Jerusalem Temple stood and sacrifices were offered there. That's all that really mattered.

The centrality of the Jerusalem Temple explains to a large extent why the Pharisees never really had much power while the Jerusalem Temple stood. There are different figures regarding how many Pharisees existed in the Late Second Temple period, but most scholars are reluctant to cite a number over 20,000, which is relatively a small number. The weak position of the Pharisees in the Late Second Temple period is confirmed in the New Testament, where the Pharisees do not seem to play a major role in the Sanhedrin, which is equivalent to the US Senate and the US Supreme Court rolled up into one for the Jews of the Late Second Temple period. Furthermore, in conflicts with the priestly class, the Pharisees almost always suffered serious casualties. One example of this was the crucifixion of 800 Pharisees by Alexander Jannaeus, a Hasomonean ruler, who being of the priestly class himself sided with the Sadducees against the Pharisees. Conflicts between the Pharisees and the Sadducees during the Hasmonean dynasty is recounted by the Jewish historian Josephus in *Jewish Antiquities* (xii, xiii). The only reason why Pharisaic Judaism became normative Judaism after the 1st century AD is because the Jerusalem Temple was completely destroyed and Jews were kicked out of Jerusalem. All priestly structures were *de facto* destroyed as a result.

While the Jerusalem Temple stood, even the Pharisees who overemphasized the Mosaic Law paid homage to the Jerusalem Temple and its cultic practice. Their lasting respect for the institution of the Jerusalem Temple is visible in the significant attention shown it in later Rabbinic writings, particularly the Babylonian Talmud. Likewise, the Qumran community respected in theory the institution of the Jerusalem Temple. They just had problems with the current leadership of the Jerusalem Temple, namely Hasmonean priests. In fact, it would not be an exaggeration to state that in the Late Second Temple period, Jerusalem Temple was held up to be the most important Jewish symbol by all who thought of themselves as Jewish.

In this environment of community value focused on the Jerusalem Temple, it is easy to see how the key signifier of "forever" triggered the desire and action toward proper cultic worship in the Jerusalem Temple. In this regard, the poet of Psalms of Solomon understood his audience and intentionally used the key signifier of "forever" to produce proper cultic worship at the Jerusalem Temple. Psalms of Solomon as a whole shows that the poet was not ignorant about the abuses that were going on in the Jerusalem Temple, even among those who were supposed to be safeguarding the purity of the Jerusalem Temple cult. In fact, the very call to God for mercy that ends Psalms of Solomon 11 shows that the poet was aware of the liability of Jews as a people for breaking their cultic obligations.

In this light, Psalms of Solomon 11 can be seen as a reformist work of liturgy composed by the poet to effectuate positive change toward proper and purer Jerusalem Temple cult observance. Although it is difficult to assess the extent to which Psalms of Solomon was read or recited by Jews of the Late Second Temple period, this does not mean that the composer of Psalms of Solomon 11 did not aspire to liturgical usage of his poem in cultic and religious settings. The poet imitated the style of Biblical Psalms in the hope of playing an important role in helping to reform the Jerusalem Temple cult of his time that was riddled with problems. The key signifier of "forever" epitomizes the poet's reformist hope.

In this chapter, we have examined the use of the key signifier of "forever" in Psalms of Solomon 11. In the process of discussion, we identified the semantic and experiential field of collective memory. We pointed to the Abrahamic covenant and its development and impact in Old Testament literature, such as in Deuteronomy 29, which functioned as a commentary, or *gemara*, on the Abrahamic covenant. We also examined the historical setting of the Psalms of Solomon in an effort to understand the world of the composer and his audience and. This was necessary in order to identify the action that the poet was trying to trigger based on the collective memory of the Abrahamic covenant.

Chapter 4

African-American Literature

Key signifier is a literary device and as such it can be applied in any literary context. Put it another way, key signifiers can be found in every genre of literature. It is possible that some writers use it without being consciously aware. It's like using a simile or metaphor. Writers can use them consciously or unconsciously in writing. Even before the literary devices of simile and metaphor were identified, writers were using them. This is clear from writings from the ancient world as well as writing from non-western worlds. Just because a literary device is not identified, it does not mean that it does not exist.

This book represents a definitive effort to define the literary device of the key signifier and identify it attested in literature. We have done so with Biblical literature and the Pseudepigrapha in the last two chapters. In this chapter, we will examine African-American literature and show how the literary device of the key signifier operates in this genre of literature. As before, the best way to approach such a study is through examination of a specific text. As we engage in the investigation of the specifics related to the key signifier in an African-American text together, we can see how we can go about identifying key signifiers in other African-American literary works. The text I have chosen for this purpose is Toni Morrison's *Beloved*.

Toni Morrison is widely recognized as an important literary figure. In 1993, she was awarded the Nobel Prize in Literature. And she has received many other literary prizes, including the Pulitzer Prize and the National Book Critics

94

Circle Award. Currently, Toni Morrison is the Robert F. Goheen Professor of Humanities at Princeton University. It is fortunate this great literary figure has decided to focus on African-American experience as her literary axis. Professor Morrison has given the world many great literary works, and the world has come closer to understanding the African-American community and the African-American experience. *Beloved* is considered Toni Morrison's greatest achievement, and it is not surprising why when one reads the novel. In my opinion, it best epitomizes African-American literature. Investigating this magnum opus will open doors to other African-American literary works.

Although many readers are aware of the story, it would be helpful to describe it briefly here. *Beloved* is a story about Beloved, who is a ghost of the child murdered by her own mother, Sethe. We find out later in the story that Sethe killed her own daughter to protect her from falling into the hands of white slave owners, because Sethe considered that worse than death. It is 1873, and Beloved, the ghost, has been rattling Sethe's house for some time. By then, Sethe and her daughter Denver were the only ones from the family living in the house. Baby Suggs, the grandmother was dead, and Sethe's two sons, Howard and Buglar, had run away from home by the time they were thirteen years old. But in 1873, Beloved takes a human form and enters into the home of Sethe and Denver. Sethe's lover Paul D was resident at the house at that time. Beloved and Denver become friends, and gradually Denver discovers who Beloved is – her dead sister come alive. Eventually, Sethe also discovers who Beloved is. As the story develops, we find a lot of background information – about slavery days and years after slavery ended. There is a historical novel nature to the accounts of mini episodes and descriptions of community actions. One disturbing event that we find is that when white slave owners tracked Sethe down and came to reclaim her, none of her African-American neighbors warned her. And they continue to hold a grudge against her for killing her own daughter. But slowly Sethe's neighbors come to realize why Sethe did what she did. As Beloved reveals herself to Sethe, tensions grow. And in the climax of tensions, Beloved seeks to kill Sethe. It is then the community realizes that Beloved is the evil spirit of Sethe's dead daughter. At the critical time, they come to rescue Sethe. In the act of redemption, the African-American community bound itself in unity. And Paul D, who also was troubled when he found about Sethe having killed her own daughter, came to realize that it was slavery which was evil and not Sethe, and he comes to support Sethe at the critical moment as well. Thus, the story ends on a happy ending. However, all's not happy in the end because there is the memory of the tragedy of a mother who is compelled to kill her daughter because she wants to protect her from the evils of slavery by white slave owners. The novel ends with the line – "It was not a story to pass on" – ringing in the reader's mind.

There is no doubt *Beloved* is a very powerful novel. Not only is it valuable as a work of literature, it opens up the semantic and experiential collective memory of the African-American community deeply affected by hundred years of slavery. As such, this book is particularly well-suited to investigating the operation of key signifiers in African-American literature. I would identify Beloved as the chief key signifier in the novel. In the following paragraph, we will examine how Beloved is the key signifier of Toni Morrison's magnum opus.

In order to understand "Beloved" as a key signifier, it is important to understand the significance of "Beloved." Toni Morrison herself has a quote from the Bible in the beginning of her novel. Since it is a quote that she herself chose, it can shed some light on "Beloved." The Bible verse is Romans 9:25, which reads: "I will call them my people, which were not my people; and her beloved, which was not beloved." We are to understand that the name Beloved was inspired by this Bible passage. This Bible verse is interesting in that it epitomizes Toni Morrison's novel in a way. Let me explain.

In *Beloved*, Toni Morrison's character Sethe is without a people in a way. When the white slave owners come to reclaim Sethe, her fellow African-

Ameicans do not warn her, knowing that she would be reclaimed by the white slave owners. African-Americans understood that they owed other African-Americans this much regardless of how close (or "far") they were. It was something that one did for one's people. But African-American neighbors did not extend this basic courtesy to Sethe. Whatever the reason may have been, it was tantamount to saying that they did not consider her a part of their people. Despite this history which isolated Sethe from the African-American community, towards the end of the novel Sethe's African-American neighbors realize their wrong and come to help Sethe as a community. It was a way of affirming Sethe as a part of the African-American community. They were, in effect, saying that Sethe was a part of their people. Thus, Sethe came to call her African-American neighbors her people because they came together to rescue her, although they were not her people in the past because they let her be reclaimed by white slave owners.

In the same way the first part of Romans 9:25 finds congruence in the story, the second part of the verse finds correlation in the novel. Sethe came to call her daughter "Beloved" by name as the ghost took on human form and lived in Sethe's house. Having died young, Sethe's daughter did not have the opportunity to be beloved. And certainly, when she was a ghost rattling Sethe's home, she was not beloved, either. But when the ghost took on human form, she had a name. That name was "Beloved." Thus, Sethe called her Beloved when she was not beloved before.

For Toni Morrison, therefore, "Beloved" held a special significance. In fact, Beloved represented the horrors of slavery. A daughter could not enjoy her mother's love because the horrors of slavery weighed heavily on the mother, who felt compelled to kill her own daughter to protect her from white slave owners and what they might do to her in the future. This was the story of Beloved. And Beloved was not alone. There were others who suffered the similar fate of Beloved.

What's more, Beloved represented all who died before their time as the result of slavery. We get an indication of this in the fact that Toni Morrison dedicated the novel to "Sixty Million and more." This figure referred to all Africans who were killed as captives in Africa awaiting the slave ship to carry them to America or died onboard the slave ship.[6] Like them, Beloved did not make it to slavery because she died. In a real sense, therefore, Beloved was one of the "Sixty Million and more."

Thus, "Beloved" embodied all the evils of slavery – the potential for Africans to die prematurely awaiting horrors of slavery, the horrors of slavery itself, and the potential of the effects of slavery to drive the African-American people apart. In this sense, we can say that "Beloved" is a key signifier because it recalls the painful collective memory of the horrors of slavery and its evil potential to destroy individual African-Americans, African-American families, and the African-American community.

A very interesting thing about this key signifier is that it is a key signifier created artificially by the author. We understand the key signifier of Beloved recalling the collective memory of the horrors of slavery because Beloved has been given identity as the embodiment of the horrors of slavery by the author of the novel. Without the novel, there would not be a semantic referencing between "Beloved" and the collective memory of the horrors of slavery. Simply put, it was Toni Morrison who created the key signifier of "Beloved."

Why is this fact significant? It is significant in our effort to understand the nature and function of key signifiers. The key signifiers studied so far were received key signifiers. What I mean by this is that they were already a part of the literary tradition and the collective memory to which referencing was done. For instance, "up to half my kingdom" was not created by the Gospel of Mark or its writer, it was already existent and functioning as a key signifier on the basis of its important role in the book of Esther and the Purim tradition. Likewise, the key

---

[6] Terry Otten, *The Crime of Innocence in the Fiction of Toni Morrison* (Columbia: University of Missouri Press, 1989), p. 83.

signifier of "forever" was not created by the poet of Psalms of Solomon. It was pre-existent vis-à-vis the composition of Psalms of Solomon 11. "Forever" was an essential part of the Abrahamic covenant, found in Genesis 17. Old Testament literary traditions built on this foundational text and the key signifier was operating based on the foundational text – either negatively or positively. Thus, as with the key signifier of "up to half my kingdom," the key signifier of "forever" was not created but was merely used based on its already important place in the collective memory of the audience. With Toni Morrison's "Beloved," it's a completely different ballgame.

Toni Morrison created "Beloved" as a key signifier to consciously refer to the horrors of slavery. Her novel's characters, plot, and discourses all contributed to the creation of the key signifier of "Beloved" with its particular purpose. In fact, I would state that Toni Morrison's creation of the key signifier of "Beloved" represents perhaps the greatest example of this kind of key signifier – a generated key signifier. And it works very well as a literary device as key signifiers are intended to work.

It is important at this juncture to point out that received key signifiers are not confined to Biblical literature or the Apocrypha and the Pseudepigrapha. Likewise, generated key signifiers are not confined to African-American literature. It is possible to find a generated key signifier in the corpus of Biblical literature and the body of literary texts referred to in the category of the Apocrypha and the Pseudepigrapha. In the same way, it is possible to find received key signifiers in African-American literature. It is important to remember that the key signifier is a literary device. And as a literary device key signifiers can have their particular characteristics.

It can be likened to the fact that we can signal a simile with either "like" or "as." Either one of the simile indicators will mark a literary structure as a simile. This can happen across all genres of literature. In the same way, received key signifiers are one type of key signifiers, and generated key signifiers are another type of key signifiers. In the next chapter, we will discuss inter-cultural key signifiers. They are another type of key signifiers. We will leave the discussion about inter-cultural key signifier for the next chapter. What's important for us to emphasize here is that regardless of what kind of key signifier a particular key signifier is, they all share the fundamental characteristic of a dual trigger mechanism – namely, the key signifier triggers collective memory or community value in the past (or present) and then triggers an action on the part of listeners or readers based on the first triggering.

This is the case with the generated key signifier of "Beloved" as found in Toni Morrison's novel. We have examined what semantic and experiential referent of collective memory "Beloved" triggered. Now, we will discuss the second triggering in the dual triggering that is fundamentally the nature of the key signifier. What is the second trigger of the key signifier of "Beloved"? In other words, what action does the key signifier compel as the result of the collective memory it recalled?

The key signifier of "Beloved" prompts an action toward communal unity. Beloved reminded African-American readers of the horrors of slavery and the divisive effect of slavery. Families were separated from one another based on the whim of slave traders and slave owners. Young healthy individuals were plucked from their homes in Africa and sold as slaves in America never to see their family or home again. Slavery was primarily about the damage to the individual and the community made up of free individuals. African communities were broken up. And during the course of slavery, there was not really a stable African-American community *qua* community.

There are many accounts of abuse of slaves by slave owners. Male slave owners felt that they had the right to do with their "property" as they pleased, and many took advantage of the situation to rape African-American women. Male slave owners had sex with African-American female slaves even though they were married and the husband was around. Both the African-American husband

and wife were thought to be the possession of the slave owner, so many were treated worse than animals. Families were broken up and an emotional strain created. Obviously, if a male slave owner goes in and have sex with a wife of one of his male slaves, it will affect the feelings of the husband toward the wife. Even if he knows that there was no fault of hers involved, the knowledge that his one and only wife had sex with another man would have been difficult to bear.

Furthermore, there was helplessness attached to it all. Even if the African-American male was big and strong and could easily defend his wife from being forced to have sex with the slave owner, he could not do anything. It could have meant not only his death, but also the death of his wife, children and other family members. The hands of the African-American male were tied from defending his wife whom he could have physically defended had he not been considered chattel.

There was a forced emotional division between the husband and the wife as the result of the rape by the slave owner. And like in many cases of rape, the victims could have felt that they were to blame. It is possible for the wife to blame the husband for not doing anything to stop the rape. Of course, she would have known that her husband really could not have done anything. But it is one thing to know cognitively a reality, it's something completely another for someone to feel personally about something. Head knowledge does not always agree with the heart or one's feelings.

Thus, there was real division created as the result of slavery as well as emotional and psychological divisions. All this contributed to the disunity among African-Americans. Furthermore, the desire to divide and control by the slave owners created active programs to keep the slave communities divided against itself. Even after slavery ended, such forces put in motion pulling members of the African-American community apart were not easily overcome.

Toni Morrison's novel effectively captures the damaging and divisive effect of the horrors of slavery. Brian Finney writes: "Ultimately the novel is about the haunting of the entire Black race by the inhuman experience of slavery, about the damage it did to their collective psyche...."[7] Thus, it is not surprising that the action sought by the key signifier of "Beloved" is to fix the problem of division that is destroying the African-American community and individuals in it.

Thus, it is not surprising that in the narrative context of the generated key signifier, the ending is a happy one. The African-American community which had shunned Sethe and didn't even help her against her slave owners eventually came to help her and united on her behalf. They, in effect, brought Sethe back into their community as one of its members. All this was because of Beloved.

In a sense, the dual triggering function of the generated key signifier of "Beloved" is represented in the plot that concerns the relationship between Sethe and the African-American community. The African-American community rejected Sethe because she had killed her own daughter. But when Beloved entered the plot, she ended up compelling the African-American community to fix up their division and hostility toward Seth and act to bring about unity of the African-American community. The final trigger function of the generated key signifier of "Beloved" was achieved on the narrative level, thereby showing the audience that this kind of work toward unity was expected.

"Beloved" functioned as a generated key signifier in the plot relating to the relationship between Sethe and Paul D as well. When Paul D finds out that Sethe had killed her own daughter, he reacts very negatively. In fact, he takes off, and the reader is left to assume at that stage of plot that he may have left for good. Division between Sethe and her lover was effectuated. Why? Because of the horrors of slavery, which caused the death of Sethe's daughter. But as with the case with the African-American community, Paul D changed his mind about Sethe. Paul D realized the horrors of slavery and understood why Sethe did what she did. His realization was effectuated by Beloved and what she represented. When Beloved attacked Sethe, it was like a mythic reliving of the horrors of

---

[7] Brian Finney, "Temporal Defamiliarization in Toni Morrison's *Beloved*," *Critical Essays on Toni Morrison's Beloved*, ed. Barbara H. Solomon (New York: G. K. Hall & Co., 1998, pp. 104-116), p. 115.

slavery attacking Sethe. Paul D realized through the generated key signifier of "Beloved" that what he should do is act toward unity. And that's what he did. And the story ends with his uniting with Sethe.

Thus, on a micro-plot level, we see two plot lines that show the reader what is the intended second trigger of the generated key signifier of "Beloved." Beloved compels the African-American community toward unity and solidarity with Sethe. And Beloved compels Paul D to unite with Sethe in solidarity and love. Thus, we can see this as a model for unity on a personal relationship level and solidarity on an African-American community level. As described above, these two areas were affected by slavery. Slavery and slave owners had a vested interested in driving a wedge of division both in the personal realm and on the community realm for African-Americans. Wendy Harding and Jacky Martin write: "In *Beloved*, Morrison once again considers the divisions threatening individual and community, but within a setting where they are both hyperdefined and in urgent need of reconciliation. The novel's community had survived the mutilating separations imposed under the brutal institution of slavery, and in the course of the novel they confront the aftermath of this institutionalized oppression."[8]

Tony Morrison has paid attention to every detail of the generated key signifier of "Beloved." She knew what semantic and experiental referents to collective memory she was inciting. And she knew what action she wanted to prompt in her readers through the key signifier of "Beloved." Her generated key signifier in the context of her novel provides guidance and direction. It is no surprise why Toni Morrison won so many awards for her novel. *Beloved* is a masterpiece of epic proportions that is a testimony to the effective working of the key signifier as a literary device.

---

[8] Wendy Harding and Jacky Martin, *A World of Difference: An Inter-Cultural Study of Toni Morrison's Novels* (Westport: Greenwood Press, 1994), p. 78.

Chapter 5

Inter-Cultural Key Signifiers

The key signifier, as a literary device, can be used across cultural and national boundaries. It can be likened to the use of the simile in this regard. You can use the simile of the Great Wall of China in your writing. For instance, you can write something like: "She crossed the street in downtown Los Angeles and beheld what looked like the Great Wall of China in front of her." Clearly, the Great Wall of China is in China and not in the United Sates of America. But it is possible to write literature using literary device referring to something that is outside of one's culture and even national boundary.

In the same way, key signifiers can refer to something outside of one's culture and one's national boundaries. One such case is found in a poem by Ai Qing of China, entitled "Mao Zedong." As the title indicates the poem was written, at least on a surface level, in praise of the famous Chinese leader. The poem was recited by the poet in China on November 6, 1941, during the Assembly of Representatives of the Shaanxi-Gansu-Ningxia Border Region. Given the context of the recital and the purpose for which it was written, the reader may assume that the primary purpose of the poem was to praise the Communist leader. On the surface level, this may be the case, but when examined carefully, the poem will reveal that Ai Qing utilized key signifiers. As we call, the key signifier is a literary device meant to recall significant idea, concepts, experiences to spur the intended audience to action. Here is Ai Qing's poem, entitled "Mao Zedong":

"Mao Zedong"[9]
by Ai Qing

Wherever Mao Zedong appears
Thunderous applause fills the air –

"The people's leader" – not a hollow term of praise;
He wins the people's trust by giving them his love.

He takes root in this vast and ancient land of China,
Bearing history's chronicles upon his own back.

Worry often spreads across his face,
His eyes reflect the people's misery.

Statesman, poet, military commander,
Revolutionary – applying thought to action;

Always pondering, always summarizing,
One hand casting aside the enemy, the other receiving more friends;

"Concentration" is his ingenious strategy –
Focussing the greatest force on the biggest enemy,

A new slogan determines a new direction:
"Give your all for the death of Fascism!"

---

[9] Ai Qing, *Selected Poems*, translated by Eugene Chen Eoyang, Peng Wenlan, and Merilyn Chin (Beijing: Foreign Language Press, 1982), p. 125.

As is clear from the surface reading of the text (what the Jewish Rabbis from the Middle Ages call "*pashat*"), it seems like a *bona fide* encomium of the Communist leader. However, a closer reading of the poem will reveal that there are important key signifiers operating.

In order to understand Ai Qing's use of key signifiers, it is important to understand something about his life. Ai Qing was born in 1910 in the mountains in Zhejiang Province of China. He was nine years old at the time of the May 4th Movement (1919). Regarding that time Ai Qing writes: "Our primary school textbook contained some enlightening views demanding democracy and science." [10] After graduating from high school in 1928, Ai Qing passed the entrance exam for the Painting Department of the West Lake National School for Fine Arts (now known as the Hangzhou Academy of Fine Arts). But before the end of the first semester, the dean of the school encouraged him to go study abroad. Ai Qing, therefore, left for Paris. He was in Paris from 1929-1932. During much of that time, Ai Qing was a penniless student in Paris and survived by working at a small arts and crafts factory. Regarding his three years in Paris, Qing writes: "In short, in my three years in Paris, I was a free spirit, even if I was indigent." [11] Most of the education he received, Qing received in the streets, so to speak. He went to Montparnasse during free time to learn painting and sketching at a "free art studio." He watched "banned" movies at the Lenin Hall in the worker's district of Paris. And Qing read on his own. His favorite poet was "the great Belgian" poet Emile Verhaeren (1855-1916). Regarding Verhaeren, Qing writes: "His poems left a deep impressionism on me. They sharply expose the unrestricted expansion of cities in the capitalist world and the consequent destruction of the countryside." [12] It is no coincidence that Emil Verhaeren was one of the founders of the school of Symbolism. Ai Qing's poems show deep

---

[10] Qing, *Selected Poems*, p. 3.
[11] Qing, *Selected Poems*, p. 5.
[12] Qing, *Selected Poems*, p. 5.

influence of the Symbolic school of poetry. He became so enchanted with this school of poetry that he started to write poetry on the sketchbook whenever he felt inspired to write poetry. Although he wrote poetry, he had not considered exchanging the artist's paintbrush for a pen of a poet until he arrived in China.

On January 28th, 1932, Ai Qing set out from Marseilles to return to China. He arrived in Shanghai in May and joined the League of Left-wing Artists and with them organized the Spring Soil Art Society. But the actions of his roommate changed the course of his life. His roommate happened to see Ai Qing's poem entitled "Gathering" about the meeting held in Paris by the Eastern Branch of the Great Anti-Imperialist League on their table and sent it to "The Dipper," a left-wing leaning periodical. It was published to Ai Qing's surprise and that was when he decided to devote his life entirely to literature.[13]

On July 12th, 1932, Ai Qing's Spring Soil Art Society was raided by secret police, and he and twelve other artists were arrested. The Kuomintang charged them with "subverting the government" under the new government policy of "Emergency Decree to Deal with Actions Endangering the Republic."[14] From jail, Ai Qing wrote many poems, which his lawyer smuggled out of the prison on his behalf. It was for fear of detection by the prison authorities that he started to use the penname of Ai Qing from 1933, starting with "Dayanhe –My Wet-Nurse." In October 1935, Ai Qing was released from prison, and in 1936 he published his first book of poems under the title, *Dayanhe*.[15]

Since then, Ai Qing was actively involved in poetry writing and published another volume of poems, entitled *The North*. He also worked as the editor of *The South*, which was a literary supplement of the *Guangxi Daily*. But the most significant event in Ai Qing's life was the meeting of Mao Zedong in 1941. Qing writes: "His stalwart figure and his affable smile left an indelible impression on

---

[13] Qing, *Selected Poems*, p. 6.
[14] Qing, *Selected Poems*, p. 6.
[15] Qing, *Selected Poems*, p. 7.

me."[16] In November, Ai Qing was elected as a delegate to the Assembly of Representatives of the Shaanxi-Gansu-Ningxia border region. It is in this context that the above poem was written and recited.

This biography of Ai Qing will help us better understand Ai Qing's key signifiers in his poem. As we recall, a key signifier is a word or phrase that refers to ideas or experiences in collective memory that has resonance with the targeted audience. However, a key signifier is not a mere echo in that there is an intentionality on the part of author to arouse his audience to action by the use of the key signifier, which has as its very essence such a trigger mechanism built in. Thus, an author or speaker can merely use the word in a sentence or a paragraph without the use of any other literary device, such as rhetoric, and achieve an impact because by nature a key signifier both recalls the past and prompts the audience to action by the very fact of its import for the society and the individual.

What are the key signifiers in Ai Qing's poem, "Mao Zedong"? To answer this question, it may be helpful to understand what is the collective memory to which Ai Qing refers for his key signifiers. In other words, what is the "text" to which Ai Qing refers in order to bring about an effect that is innately a part of key signifiers? What events, ideas, or experiences are shared by his audience that would allow for the use of key signifiers employed in his poem?

The "text" to which Ai Qing refers is Hitler and his Fascist program in Germany. It is a socio-cultural text for his audience because it was such a significant reality at the time. In fact, it may be argued that Hitler and Nazi Fascism were the most dominant factor at the time. It was not only the collective memory of the Chinese audience that Ai Qing was addressing. Hitler and Nazi Fascism were in the collective memory of virtually anyone in the world who cared about global politics and read news that concerned the world. Hitler and Nazism provided a text for Ai Qing to draw from because it was in the collective memory or collective experience of virtually everyone in the audience. Everyone

---

[16] Qing, *Selected Poems*, p. 8.

108

has seen the news regarding Hitler, his rise to power, his slogans, and the titles used to galvanize his people.

This is quite evident even at a first glance. In fact, Ai Qing uses the very word "Facism" in the last line of his poem. Even without the examination of his background, it is easy to see his intentioned use of this collective memory and the key role it played in his poem. Ai Qing could have just as well said, "Death to Capitalism!" or "Death to Bourgeoisie!" or some other such type of slogan. The fact that he mentioned Fascism is a clear indication that it was this "text" that was integral to his intentioned writing. In a way, Ai Qing was giving a reference point for the audience and the readers. In other words, Ai Qing was informing his readers that the symbols and ideas referred (or inferred to) in this poem are related to Nazi Fascism and Hitler.

In a way, Ai Qing was making it easier for his readers to identify the key signifiers consciously by giving this explicit clue at the end. But as key signifiers are intended to function at a collective memory level and not necessarily at the conscious level, Ai Qing did not necessarily have to give such an overt indication to have the desired effect inherent in key signifiers. In fact, I would argue that the very attack of Fascism in the last stanza, "Give your all for the death of Fascism!" was a concerted effort of Ai Qing to detract his audience. In his artistic vanity, he wanted to make people understand that the key signifiers in the poem referred to Hitler and Nazi Fascism. How could he explicitly let his audience know about his artistic referents in the context of the *peshat* ("surface reading") of the poem praising Mao Zedong? He could only do it in a form of a Communist slogan against Fascism. And that's what he did.

It is important to recognize the fact that the existence of the slogan against Fascism does not necessarily mean that Ai Qing was anti-Hitler or anti-Fascist. In fact, the "slogan" at the end is introduced by an introductory narrative-type comment that a new slogan determines a new direction. In a sense, Ai Qing was basically stating something to this effect: "I am going to state a slogan that is new and I am just repeating it." He is not being seriously committal in any way. This is an important factor to keep in mind while reading the poem. Because Ai Qing was in a Communist regime, he could not show his open sympathy for Hitler or Nazi Fascism. But he did not want to betray Hitler and Nazi Fascism, so he introduces a formulaic slogan that is anti-Fascist, rather than a direct comment from himself against Fascism or Hitler.

It is possible that there were those who shared his pro-Hitler and pro-Nazi sentiment in the audience. Chinese Communism did not have any real conflicts with Fascism as such. There was no reason for anybody to hate Hitler or Nazism. In fact, in this period, China was going through a nationalist phase, emphasizing Chinese ethnic purity and the "China for the Chinese" idea. The discourse about driving out the foreigners and non-Chinese from the land was prevalent. Chinese nationalism which fuelled Chinese Communism and virtually all Chinese movements – even those that were anti-Communist – is not unlike German nationalism and the discourse of "Germany for the Germans" that fuelled Nazism.

It was a fact that Ai Qing lived in Paris during the rise of Nazism (or proto-Nazism). Not once did he explicitly or even implicitly attack Hitler or Nazism, although he was involved with Communist movements in Paris and in China. This seems strange in light of the close proximity of Paris to Germany and also the fact that events in Germany were relevant to China. If Ai Qing really hated Hitler and Nazi Fascism, why doesn't any of his paintings or poems or writings reflect this? Had Ai Qing written anti-Nazi Fascism poems, he would not have been criticized. But Ai Qing specifically chose not to criticize Hitler and Nazism.

This encomium to Mao Zedong, in fact, is a veiled praise of Hitler and Nazism. Most probably, Ai Qing bought into and sympathized with Hitler and the Nazi program because they mirrored what Chinese nationalists tried to accomplish in the Chinese context, albeit via the use of a different political

110

philosophy. In other words, the goals were the same and that was what attracted Ai Qing to Hitler and Nazism.

Indeed, the poem "Mao Zedong" contains many references to Hitler and Nazism. Even the first two lines, where applause fills the air wherever Mao Zedong appears is more reminiscent of Hitler. Who can forget the TV scenes of Hitler appearing amid tremendous amount of applause. Such TV scenes were broadcast throughout the world. They were written about in newspapers around the world. Ai Qing would have had opportunities to see such images frequently. Wherever Hitler appeared, applause filled the air.

Ai Qing only met Mao Zedong for the first time in 1941, and he wrote his poem praising Mao Zedong in the same year. His previous writings do not show an explicit adoration of Mao Zedong. More importantly, Ai Qing did not have opportunities to see Mao Zedong appearing in many places and receiving the applause of the people. The imagery invoked in the first two stanzas is of Hitler rather than of Mao Zedong. Ai Qing was exposed to the kind of adoration Hitler received wherever he went for years and years. He was not exposed to such images of Mao Zedong in the year he wrote the poem after meeting Mao Zedong for the first time in 1941.

The reality that Ai Qing was referring to Hitler rather than Mao Zedong is reinforced throughout the poem. In the next stanza (3rd line in the poem), Ai Qing mentioned the title "The people's leader." This title is the exact title that was applied to Hitler. Germans referred to Hitler as the leader (*Fuhrer*) of the people (*das Volk*). In contrast, Mao Zedong's typtical title was not "the people's leader". The specific use of the primary title for Hitler in the German context is clear evidence that this poem by Ai Qing was meant to be a veiled encomium for Hitler and although in *peshat* (surface reading), it was an encomium of Mao Zedong.

The third stanza also proves that this poem was meant to be an encomium to Hitler. The third stanza reads: "He takes root in this vast and ancient land of China,/

Bearing history's chronicles upon his own back." Clearly, this cannot apply to Mao Zedong. Mao Zedong was a Chinese nationalist who wanted China for the Chinese people. However, Mao Zedong was not interested in connecting to the Chinese past history *per se*. He was interested more in building up a New China. And, in a sense, this is compatible with Communism. Marxist program is, in fact, a kind of Hegelian dialectic experience to produce a new reality.

Hitler and Nazism were different. Hitler's nationalist program was not discontinuous or dialectic along consciously Hegelian lines. Hitler and Nazism envisioned a direct connection to the past. Hitler and Nazism read German history as continuous and argued that the German people had an obligation to build on the past. The very fact that Hitler and Nazis called their rule "The Third Reich" is a clear evidence of their building their rule upon Germany's past history. Why not call their rule "The First Reich" or "The Greatest Reich"? Hitler and Nazism consciously built their political program on the backs of Germany's past history. Mao Zedong did not do this at all. Thus, it was Hitler who carried history's chronicles on his own back. It was Hitler who glorified the German past as an integral part of his political ideology and program. It was Hitler who emphasized Germany as an ancient land with a magnificent past. It was Hitler who rooted himself in Germany's past. Mao Zedong does not fit the image outlined in the third stanza of Ai Qing's poem.

The sixth stanza further proves that Ai Qing had Hitler as his hero and praised him in this poem. The sixth stanza reads: "Always pondering, always summarizing, / One hand casting aside the enemy, the other receiving more friends." This stanza refers to the typical Nazi wave that characterized Hitler's speeches. Hitler raised his right hand to give a Nazi salute and it represented for Ai Qing a casting aside of his enemies. As Hitler's right hand was held high, pushing away his political enemies and those who opposed Nazism in Germany, his other hand (the left hand) stood at his side, symbolizing more and more people who came to side with him as time went on. Ai Qing shows respect for Hitler's speeches which were often seen as summarizing German history for the masses and giving complex instructions for the German people in pithy, formulaic sentences.

The seventh stanza shows that Ai Qing's respect for Hitler was not limited to his peaceful political activities, such as giving speeches, but also to his signature program that was filled with violence and death – namely, the concentration camp. The seventh stanza proclaims: ""Concentration" is his ingenious strategy – / Focussing the greatest force on the biggest enemy". The seventh stanza shows that Ai Qing had a great admiration for Hitler's program of putting Jews in concentration camps. "Concentration" was not any of the strategies of Mao Zedong, but it was a central strategy of Hitler and Nazi Germany. Ai Qing describes the strategy of putting Jews in concentration camps as "ingenious." And the seventh stanza also makes it clear why Ai Qing thought that this program of Hitler was ingenious. Ai Qing praises focusing the greatest force on the biggest enemy. The concentration camps allowed Hitler to do this. Hitler identified Jews as the greatest enemy for Germany and its national security. The rationale of Hitler was that Jews posed an internal threat that weakened the very fabric of the German society and the viability of Germany as a nation. After identifying Jews as the greatest enemy of Germany, Hitler systematically put Jews in concentration camps. Concentration camps taxed German resources and forces. Ai Qing praises this as a good move on Hitler's part.

It is important to recall that Ai Qing was in Paris from 1929-1932. Certainly, Ai Qing was aware of the Jewish Question being debated at the time and the force of Zionism in Europe. In fact, Paris was one of the main intellectual centers of Zionism and many Zionists spent their time in Paris both in Jewish contexts and non-Jewish, general setting of Paris, to debate the Jewish Question. After all, Napoleon himself had convened the Great Sanhedrin made of Jewish rabbis and influential Jewish laymen to discuss the issue of Jewish identity on January 20, 1807. The quest for Jewish identity has been at the heart of the

Jewish experience in Paris since then and it was no different at the time of Ai Qing. An intellectual like Ai Qing, who ran around in artistic places, was surely aware of the Jewish Question. Certainly, the intellectuals he read had interest in such issues at that time. And there were many pamphlets and writings written both by Zionists and those who opposed Zionism at that time in Paris, which Ai Qing was exposed to just by being in Paris in artistic circles for several years. It is clear from this poem where Ai Qing came down. He was sympathetic to Hitler and those who opposed Zionism and the Jews.

The internal evidence of "Mao Zedong" clearly point to the identity of this poem as Ai Qing's veiled encomium to Hitler and Nazism. Of course, in the context of Communist China, he could not openly praise Hitler and Nazism. After all, Fascism, at least on paper, was seen as the direct enemy of Communism in the political ideological spectrum. For the same reason, Ai Qing probably hid his pro-Hitler and pro-Nazi sentiments. Even exposure of anti-Jewish sentiment could be construed as pro-Fascism sentiment and could have been manipulated by his enemies. He had spent time in jail for supposedly being anti-government and he was not about to put himself in such a predicament again. It was in his interest to hide anything that resembled any movement that could have been construed as anti-Communist in any way. At least at the level of *peshat* (surface reading), Ai Qing had to keep things "kosher". But that did not prevent Ai Qing from utilizing a kind of *Animal Farm* type praise of Hitler and Nazism. The fact that Ai Qing did this in the poem, etitled "Mao Zedong," is ingenious because who would arrest him for a poem entitled "Mao Zedong" even if people know that it was a veiled praise for Hitler and Nazism? "Literally" it was towing the line of praising Mao Zedong. It kept the letter of the law and no one could fault Ai Qing on that. In fact, most likely, Ai Qing could not have written anything that even resembled praise of Hitler or Nazism in any other poem. They could have called him up on charges. But no one would have dared to do that with the poem praising Mao Zedong.

This is the precise genius of Ai Qing. As an experienced artist and poet, who had suffered in jail at the hand of a government which mistrusted his writings, he devised a way to express his true self in an artistic way that neither compromised his artistic truth or personal self nor made him culpable to the state. In fact, Ai Qing lived a long life and was celebrated as a Communist poet *par excellence*. He was celebrated by the state. Ironically enough, such celebrity Ai Qing enjoyed owed much to his poem praising Mao Zedong. Perhaps, it can be said that Ai Qing's life represents his greatest artistic masterpiece. Ai Qing managed to use his training in Symbolism style of poetry to veil his true self while testifying to it with loud speakers through artistic devices and his artistic and poetic work, while receiving support from people and the state who may have found his fully unveiled ideas a threat to the Communist state.

If it is the case that Ai Qing's adoration of Hitler and Nazism was a threat to the Communist state, then how could his poem contain key signifiers? Key signifiers, by nature, prompt the audience or the reader to action. But this is the beauty of the literary device of the key signifier. It works primarily on a collective memory level and often this is at an unconscious level and not a conscious one. Of course, an in-depth literary criticism can dissect the process but literary analysis informs on a critical level. Such criticism is not necessary to achieve the literary effect of the key signifier intended by the author or poet.

A good illustration of the idea that literary criticism or understanding of literary tools is not necessary for the reader to be impacted by the literary device is found in the example of the simile. Let us use the same simile and the example mentioned in the beginning of the chapter: "She crossed the street in downtown Los Angeles and beheld what looked like the Great Wall of China in front of her." Of course, those who have studied the literary device of the simile can argue that "like the Great Wall of China" is a simile. This person can also dissect and explain what this means and the implication of this. But this expertise is unnecessary to appreciate the literary device of the simile and be affected by it.

For instance, a person with an elementary education and no high school education can read the whole sentence and understand that she stood in front of a tall and long wall. The minimally educated reader may have seen the Great Wall of China on a TV special and know what it is. And as long as he has this collective memory of the Great Wall of China shared by many people he can understand the sentence and the meaning conveyed by the sentence without knowing what a simile is or what a simile does. The key signifier is the same The reader or the audience does not need to understand or be able to explain what a key signifier is to be impacted by it in the poem that he reads or a speech he hears. It's a literary device like the simile. It can be used consciously and it can even be used unconsciously and unknowingly by the speaker or the writer.

Key signifiers in Ai Qing's poem, "Mao Zedong," functions on the same level. Like all key signifiers, they draw on a text from the collective memory of the readers. There is an intentionality built into the key signifiers themselves of producing a result or effect. What are the key signifiers in Ai Qing's poem, "Mao Zedong"? There are two major key signifiers in the poem; namely, "The People's Leader" in stanza 2 and "concentration" in stanza 7. How do they function as key signifiers?

First, I will discuss the key signifier of "The People's Leader" in stanza 2. For Ai Qing's audience, the phrase, "The People's Leader," was a familiar one. In other words, this was a title that was in the collective memory and collective consciousness of the Chinese people. Why was this the case? Hitler and Nazism was the most prominent global reality at the time of the composition of "Mao Zedong" by Ai Qing. Everyone around the world who had a TV or radio or read newspapers were aware of the title "The People's Leader" attached to Hitler and Nazism. The title bringing together two key words in Nazism (*Fuhrer* and *Volk*), which in a sense epitomized Hitler and Nazism.

The phrase, "The People's Leader," is a key signifier because it recalled a collective memory. Albeit being a short phrase, it referred to a whole system or a world of ideas and experiences. The title would have immediately invoked Hitler and Nazism that was attached to Hitler. The key signifier would open the door to the world that was represented by them. In this regard, the phrase "The People's Leader" can be seen as an example of an inter-cultural usage of key signifiers.

Obviously, Chinese culture is different from German culture. Chinese experiences are different from German experiences. Historically, Chinese philosophy and religion are different from those of German ones. To a large extent, it would be fair to say that the Chinese worldview – both on individual and collective levels – is different from the German worldview. Then, how is it possible to talk about key signifiers across cultures? The phrase, "The People's Leader," provides a concrete picture into this reality.

If we recall, a key signifier is a word or phrase that recalls a collective memory. Often, a people's collective memory is based on the history of that people. In other words, key signifiers often function diachronically. Thus, it would be expected for Chinese people at the time of Ai Qing's time to be influenced more by their own past history. Collective memory of the Chinese people at Ai Qing's time, for instance, probably incorporated common experiences in their immediate past experience, such as the Boxers' Rebellion (1900). In a similar way, the American collective memory is profoundly affected by 9/11 and the British collective memory is impacted by 7/7. Both the 9/11 terrorist attack and 7/7 terrorist attack were global news at the time of occurrence. However, with the passage of time, American collective memory will retain 9/11 whereas most Americans will forget 7/7. However, British people will not forget the London terrorist attack of 7/7.

This illustrates what makes collective memory what it is. 9/11 is more relevant to the American people because it happened to them. However, because it was a one-time experience, it may not be remembered by other peoples as starkly. Certainly, 7/7 is a good example of this. Although most Americans know 9/11, how many Americans know 7/7? Your average Joe in the street will not know the significance of 7/7 in 2006 even though it happened in London in 2005. For Americans, it is fair to say that there is no collective memory whatsoever about 7/7. It was just one event in news. In contrast, 7/7 remains in the collective memory of the British people. To be fair to Americans, it is important to mention the Madrid bombing – another terrorist incident that is only a few years old. For the Spanish people, this is in the collective memory, but for the British people, it is just a one time event that hit the news for a while, but did not remain in the British collective memory. Often, collective memory of a people is shaped by something that identifies them within the same group. Thus, 7/7 is a key signifier for the British people, whereas it would not be for Americans.

It is easy to understand why key signifier is influenced diachronically by a people. They are bound in group identity and share concerns that somehow relate to them on a group level although they may be individuals – even vastly different individuals with vastly different individual identity. Although it is true that diachronic developments often shape key signifiers, it would be wrong to rule out the potential for synchronic key signifiers.

By synchronic key signifiers, I refer to key signifiers that develop on a horizontal rather than a vertical plane in terms of human and group experience. Thus, for Ai Qing's time of 1941, the Boxers' Rebellion of 1900 represents a vertical impact. However, 1941 China was impacted by 1941 German, which is not on a vertical axis of time but rather on a horizontal axis.

And it cannot be denied that the horizontal impact (the synchronic impact) has just as much influence as the vertical impact (the diachronic impact) – certainly in terms of the audience intended to receive the key signifier. In other words, an author or a poet can use a key signifier that recalls the collective memory of his audience that is shaped by events and ideas of another (foreign) people. In the case of Ai Qing, the collective memory of his audience was impacted by Hitler and Nazism in real ways. Although Hitler and Nazism were on a horizontal (synchronic) plane and not a vertical (diachronic) one, its impact on his audience and readership was just as profound. Certainly in terms of its collective memory impact, Hitler and Nazism may have been more influential, at least for a time, than even some of the diachronic factors, such as the Boxers' Rebellion.

In other words, key signifiers drawing from Hitler and Nazism at the time of Ai Qing would have held a real significance for his Chinese audience – potentially more so than the key signifiers drawing from the Boxer's Rebellion. Several factors can be attributed to the overriding impact of Hitler and Nazism for Chinese collective memory. First of all, media has something to do with the influence. Hitler and Nazism were always in the news at the time. Secondly, the Chinese people and the German people of 1941 shared common goals and vision for their nation. Germans wanted a powerful Germany with Germans ruling the country without any outside or foreign influence. The Chinese people in 1941 wanted to command their own destiny and purify China of foreign influences. In a sense, it may not be mistaken to say that Nazism represented a reinforcement of Chinese collective values in 1941, such as the values attached to the Boxers' Rebellion and diachronic development from such Chinese nationalist movement with violent overtones. Thirdly, success of Hitler and Nazism made an impact. The Chinese had failure after failure for decades to achieve what they wanted and they were working for success in their nationalistic program. Hitler and the Nazis seemed to be effective and successful to unify the country and very successful in their war program in 1941. It is understandable why many Chinese would have admired the accomplishments of Hitler and the Nazis in 1941. Thus, Hitler's success can be seen as a contributing factor to his impact on the Chinese collective memory. These are only a few of the factors that contributed to the overriding impact of Hitler and Nazism for Chinese collective memory. But there were many other factors as well. Perhaps, one can say that it was the spirit of the age vis-à-vis the Chinese people.

Thus, the key symbols of Nazism – namely, *Fuhrer* and *Volk* – came to open the door to the Nazi world of ideas and experiences. Ai Qing as an expert poet was able to use the literary device of key signifier effectively in his poem, "Mao Zedong." Ai Qing knew that the key signifier of "The People's Leader" will open up the semantic world of Hitler and Nazism. Not only did the phrase, "The People's Leader," recall the central ideas and experiences of Hitler and Nazism, it prompted the Chinese audience to action. The important question is – what was the action being prompted by the key signifier?

To understand this, it is important to remember the aspiration of the Chinese people in 1941. China did not have any Jews, so annihilating Jews was irrelevant. All the writings of the Nazis regarding killing Jews would have had no impact on China because there were no Jews. What China wanted and was looking for in 1941 was Chinese unity and nationalism. The Chinese leaders were looking to unify China devoid of foreign influences. They wanted to be an independent, proud nation who can dictate their own destiny and future. It was this Chinese aspiration and dream that made Hitler a hero in the Chinese collective memory and which elevated Nazism to a lofty place in the Chinese collective (sub)consciousness.

It was in this historical *Sitz im Leben* of China that the key signifier of "The People's Leader" held a significant value. What did Ai Qing seek to accomplish through this key signifier? In other words, what was the intended causation of the key signifier? It is closely tied to the Chinese aspiration. Ai Qing wanted (1) to encourage Mao Zedong to be the kind of people's leader that Hitler was to the Germans, (2) to encourage the people to work toward the kind of national unity that the Nazis were able to achieve under Hitler. The impact or desired causation was possible because every Chinese person hearing this poem or reading this poem in a literary setting would be aware of the news concerning Hitler and the Nazis. In 1941, they were aware of the tremendous success that a country formerly devastated by war, factionalism, and foreign influences were able to achieve in a relatively short time. Hitler and Nazism have accomplished in the view of 1941 what Mao Zedong and the Chinese wanted to accomplish for themselves.

The key signifier of "The People's Leader" drawing on the world of Hitler and Nazism made resonance in the Chinese population of 1941 because Hitler was in the Chinese collective memory and the goals of Nazism vis-à-vis Germany closely resembled the nationalist goals of the Chinese people of 1941 for themselves. Ai Qing wanted to see a strong leadership in China and an independent and strong China. In 1941, key signifiers drawing on Hitler and Nazism could best achieve this goal.

Besides the key signifier of "The People's Leader," another inter-cultural key signifier that Ai Qing uses is "concentration" in stanza 7. Both of the key signifiers draw on Hitler and Nazism, which were an important part of the Chinese collective memory in 1941. Whereas "The People's Leader" is a key signifier building on the person of Hitler as a leader in the Nazi context, "concentration" is a key signifier that builds on the program of Nazism that Hitler pushed. Concentration camps were set up in Germany and Poland and millions of Jews were transported to concentration camps via trains. The whole program to put millions of Jews in concentration camps was an elaborate and systematic program that involved several stages.

First, Jews were identified, either by the police or by neighbors, friends, acquaintances, or by family members (via marriage). Then, these Jews were arrested and placed in local holding cells. Then, they were systematically transported by the rail system to designated concentration camps. Once at the concentration camps, these Jews were killed systematically. In this way, over 6 million Jews from all over Europe were killed. The program, while seen as ruthless, is often described as efficient and effective in attaining the goals outlined by Hitler and Nazism.

China practically had no Jews. China was not interested in an annihilationist program directed at Jews. But what China needed and desired was an efficient program to achieve its own goals. Concentration camps of Nazi Germany represented an efficient implementation of national goals, where each element of the system functioned efficiently. Nazi Germany in 1941 represented the kind of efficiency that 1941 China tried to achieve. Thus, it is not difficult to see why Nazi Germany held the imagination and collective consciousness of Chinese people at the time. Ai Qing as a poet in tune with the Chinese masses and collective memory was quick to utilize the literary tool of key signifier to achieve an effect or causality. And the causality that Ai Qing sought was to prompt the Chinese toward greater efficiency and unity in achieving the national goals of the Chinese people in 1941.

"Concentration" was an efficient key signifier for Ai Qing to utilize because it encapsulated in the collective memory of the Chinese people the efficient program of Hitler and Nazi Germany. In 1941, it was a powerful inter-cultural key signifier. Almost all of his readers and listeners would have recognized the powerful key signifier of Ai Qing's poem, "Mao Zedong." And many would have been impacted by the key signifier in the way intended by the key signifier.

A question rises. How can Ai Qing use "The People's Leader" and "concentration" as key signifiers if the literary device of the key signifier has not been identified in 1941? It is true that I am the first person to identify and define the literary device of key signifier. And the identification was made in the beginning of the 21st century. To phrase the question in another way, how can Ai Qing be using the literary device of the key signifier if he did not know of the existence of such a literary device? Ai Qing was not trained in this literary device.

To answer this question, I would refer to the literary device of the simile. It is possible to use the literary device of the simile, knowing what it is, understanding its definition and usage, and consciously structuring one's poem using the literary device of the simile. However, it is also possible to use simile without consciously using it or using it after being trained in it. For instance, it is possible for someone to have read a usage of the simile and mimicked the usage in his own writing without critically examining the literary device as such.

To better understand this reality, let us recall our example of a simile: "She crossed the street in downtown Los Angeles and beheld what looked like the Great Wall of China in front of her." Here, we see that "like the Great Wall of China" is a simile. We know this to be a simile because we have been trained in the literary device. We learned about it in school or read about in books.

But even if we do not know what the literary device of simile is, that does not mean that we are not impacted by it. We can understand that the woman in downtown Los Angeles came to behold something really big. We know that because we know that the Great Wall of China is big. We may not know exactly what she stood in front of but we know what it was like. Even if we were never taught what a simile is and never even heard of the word "simile," we experience the effect of the literary device as readers or audience.

In a similar way, it is possible to use the literary device of the simile without having learned what it is or being aware of its definition. Someone who just came from downtown Los Angeles can say to a friend, "Man, I just came back from Los Angeles, and I saw something incredible. It looked like the Great Wall of China. Remember that Discovery Channel program?" This person may not know what a simile is. He is merely describing what he saw. But he has used a literary device of simile.

The situation is applicable to our example of a simile: "She crossed the street in downtown Los Angeles and beheld what looked like the Great Wall of China in front of her." An author can write this statement without knowing what a simile is. But that does not mean that he does not achieve the goals set apart for the literary device of simile. In other words, without knowing it, the author has successfully used the literary device of the simile and achieved the effects that the literary device of the simile is to achieve.

Just like the literary device of the simile, the literary device of the key signifier functions in the same way. It is possible to use the literary device without knowing the definition or the description of usage and intended effect. But even without being aware of these important factors, the author or the poet or the speaker can accurately and effectively use the literary device of the key signifier.

This was the case with Ai Qing. Ai Qing used the key signifiers of "The People's Leader" and "concentration" in his poem, "Mao Zedong" without being aware of the definition of the key signifier, its characteristic, and intended effect. How could he have known all this since it was over 60 years after the poem that I coined the term "key signifier" as a literary device?

It is important to emphasize that like the example of simile above, it was possible to use literary devices without being aware of the critical definitions of them. In other words, it is possible or writers and speakers to utilize literary devices both consciously and unconsciously. It is also possible for writers and speakers to use literary device which have not been coined yet. Even before coining the term "simile" to describe the literary device, writers and speakers used it.

In a sense, identification and coining of a literary device *qua* literary device is the work of the literary critic, rather than the job of the artist or the poet. Of course, it is possible for the artist or the poet to be a literary critic himself, but it is not a necessary condition of being an artist or a poet. To illustrate this, look at the field of sports. Generally, coaches are those who have played sports on a professional level. But the best players do not necessarily make the best coaches. Also, a person who has never played any kind of sports can be a sports commentator or an academic analyzer of sports or a professor of sports science. Being a good athlete does not necessarily make her a good sports anchor, coach, or sports writer. In fact, a person who is not actively participating in the game of sports but is an announcer or a sports writer may better coin a term or phrase to describe events in the sports game or a type of play or action within the context of an active game. In the same way, the poet or the writer himself may not always be the best individuals to identify the "plays" of the written text or the spoken text. The poet or the artist is not always the best critic of art or poetry. There are cross-overs, but being a literary critic does not obligate the literary critic to engage in the creation of art or poetry himself. Likewise, being an artist or a poet does not obligate the artist or the poet to engage in literary criticism.

This process helps to explain how a writer or a poet can employ literary devices that have not even been coined or defined in terms of literary criticism, yet. In the case of Ai Qing's poems, this is true. And this would be true of people writing in non-western traditions using literary device coined in the west.

It is a fact of the matter that Ai Qing was a master of his craft, which is poetry. Even though he may not have had a critical definition of the key signifier before him, he used the literary device in the way that it was intended to be used along the lines of critical definition using literary criticism categories. "Mao Zedong" remains a testimony to Ai Qing's mastery of poetry. And his poem testifies to Ai Qing's place in the history of the usage of the key signifier as a literary device. And no student of the key signifier can ignore Ai Qing's poem "Mao Zedong" when studying inter-cultural usage of key signifiers.

Chapter 6

Key Signifiers in Media

The key signifier is a literary device, and as such it can be used in every literary context. Key signifiers can be used in poetry as well as in prose. Key signifiers can be used in every literary genre available in the world, regardless of culture, national boundary, or history. In fact, the key signifier is not confined to the written text. Key signifiers can be employed in speeches and in normal conversations as well just as you can use simile and metaphor in every day speech with your family and friends. As such, key signifiers can be important literary device in all kind of media related genres, including the movies.

In this chapter, we will investigate the use of key signifiers in movies. The same definition operates for movies as in written literature. Let us recall the definition: "A key signifier is defined as a term or phrase that triggers a collective memory or a community value that is over-arching and all-encompassing. A key signifier functions aggressively in the literary context to spur audience to action." Using this definition, we will identify key signifiers in movies.

But before we dive into movies, let us consider how key signifiers can be used in spoken language. Previously, we have discussed how the key signifier of "1.5 generation" in the Korean-American context can be used in a speech. Since we have some notion of how key signifiers can be used in a delivered speech, we can add to our understanding of key signifier in spoken speech by looking at more examples.

Let us look at how key signifiers are used in normal conversations. Let us suppose that Bob and John saw the movie, *The Terminator* (1984), a few days after the movie came out. The movie had a big opening weekend. Everyone in the work place was talking about the movie by water coolers. Students were talking about how cool the movie was in their lunch time. Many people share what their favorite part of the movie was. People will describe their favorite scenes. And in the course of discussion about the movie, the movie comes into the collective memory of a people. Many people reading this book will have seen the movie and can identify with what is being described. If you ask anyone today what they remember about the movie made a couple of decades ago, they will say the line, "I'll be back!" The line was uttered by Arnold Schwarzenegger in the character of The Terminator.

It may be good to recap the plot of the movie, briefly, because many of us may have forgotten the plot (although we have not forgotten the saying!). Arnold Schwarzenegger is The Terminator, a robot from the future. As an advanced cyborg, The Terminator – also referred to as Cyberdyne system model 101, a T800 – looks like a human and has fully human functions. But he's made of metal and heavy duty industrial materials from the future. He is sent back from the future to earth by the machines which become self-aware and try to destroy the humans and take over the world. These are, of course, machines that humans have created. The machines send The Terminator back into the past to kill the mother of John Connor, who is a future revolutionary leader for the humans fighting the machines. The goal of The Terminator is to kill the mother before she gives birth to John Connor.

Human beings send someone back into the past to defend John Connor's mother. He is one Kyle Reese (Michael Biehn). Kyle locates John Connor's mother, Sarah Connor (Linda Hamilton), and explains the situation to her. Eventually, Kyle convinces Sarah, and he becomes her protection against The Terminator. And The Terminator is unrelenting in his effort to kill Sarah. "I'll be back!" is found in one of these scenes where The Terminator is trying to kill Sarah. It takes place in a police station. After The Terminator says, "I will be back," he disappears and then soon afterwards reappears in the scene by crashing through the wall in a car. Sarah escapes relatively unscathed. And the movie ends on a positive note with The Terminator dead and Sarah alive to give birth to John Connor, who will save the humans in the future.

After the release of the movie, the saying – "I will be back!" – came to be identified with Arnold Schwarzenegger. And it was, interestingly enough attributed to him in a positive way. It is difficult to explain how a villain in the movie became a hero and the saying that was meant for revenge against the humans came to be a positive saying in American collective memory, but this is what happened. "I will be back!" came to have such a positive presence in the American collective memory that Arnold Schwarzenegger used the saying in his campaign trail to be the Governor of California. He received quite an applause for saying that because Americans love that saying and it has a positive collective memory. Most people today probably do not remember the context in which it was said. Many probably would tell you that it's about revenge, but they probably do not think of it as a negative thing.

Perhaps, this is a commentary on the American people. We are a people who think that revenge is not necessarily a bad thing. In fact, many Americans would use revenge and "justice" interchangeably at times. And movies that show revenge for injustice done often win audiences over and become big box office hits. Americans like to see bad guys having their butt kicked. United States President seems to have this spirit. When 9/11 hit, he called the US response, "Operation Infinite Justice." It was a euphemism for the revenge that he wanted America to extract from the culprits of 9/11. Revenge, euphemistically called "justice," is a very important part of American consciousness. And somehow, the saying "I will be back!" came to be fixed in the collective memory of Americans along this line.

The case was not so different even immediately after the movie came out. People were going around and saying, "I will be back!" And often, it was meant in a positive sense of delivering justice. So, it seems that the current collective memory regarding "I will be back!" was fixed soon after the release of the film. Bob and John, our imaginary characters who saw the movie *The Terminator* soon after it came out, would have been a part of that collective memory.

Let us suppose that Bob and John were engaged in a conversation soon after they saw the movie. Somehow the conversation turned into an argument. John became so mad that he dashes off. But before he leaves the room, he says, "I will be back!" Bob would have known what he was saying and what he was referring to. Anyone who was in the room would have perceived similarly if they had seen the movie by Arnold Schwarzenegger.

John has used the phrase, "I will be back," as a key signifier. As we recall, the key signifier has a dual triggering mechanism. On the one hand, it triggers collective memory or community value, and on the other hand, it triggers an action on the audience. In this light, what is the dual triggering mechanism of the key signifier of "I will be back"?

First of all, we know that collective memory that John is describing. It is the collective memory of the positive content of righteous revenge that came to be associated with "I will be back!" In a sense, the audience would have had this collective memory even if they had not seen the film. "I will be back" became ubiquitous. Thus, even Fundamentalist Christians who never see Rated-R films would be part of the collective memory of Americans who understand the referent content meaning of "I will be back." It recalls the collective memory based on the movie. But in a sense, the collective memory has taken a life of its own. Saying "I will be back" in the American context, therefore, does not necessarily recall the movie *The Terminator* but rather the collective memory that came out of that movie and came to be imbedded in the American psyche. And this collective memory, which is being triggered, is of righteous revenge.

What is the other element triggered by the key signifier of "I will be back"? In other words, what action from the audience is the key signifier meant to trigger? In the context of John and Bob, John intended to cause Bob to fear some kind of retaliation or revenge. The action intended by the key signifier of "I will be back!" is fear.

In a sense, when Arnold Schwarzenegger said, "I will be back!" during his political campaign, he was using it as a key signifier. The key signifier of "I will be back!" recalled the American collective memory of a righteous revenge or an upright struggle to make things right again. This was one of the dual triggers. The other trigger was that Arnold Schwarzenegger wanted to produce fear in those who were running against him. In this sense, Arnold Schwarzenegger's use of the key signifier of "I will be back!" is qualitatively similar to John's use of the key signifier in his altercation with Bob.

As we can see, key signifiers can be used in conversations as well as in speech. Let us consider another example to further illustrate the use of key signifiers in popular speech and conversation. Let us suppose that a father took his daughter and her boyfriend for some ice cream at a local Dairy Queen. The father never really liked the boy friend but he loves his daughter. He is not such a bad guy but the father feels that he is not good enough for his daughter. The father thinks that there are dozens of other guys who are better qualified to be her mate.

The daughter has been dating the guy for a few months and considers him a serious boyfriend. She is thinking of a future with him. Although a senior in high school, she is thinking about a marriage in a few years potentially with him. She thinks she's in love. Being a senior she applied to several colleges. She applied for a college near home, which was not her first choice but has a good academic program. She also applied to a number of other colleges that she preferred to attend instead. Her first choice was Williams College in Massachusetts. Being in top of her class academically, she was accepted by

Williams College, her first choice school. She had applied to study English and desired to be a writer in the future. She was accepted at a local college, but it does not have the reputation that Williams has in producing great writers.

Her boyfriend is not as academically inclined as her. He is, in fact, a class clown and quite funny. He is good natured and a decent person, and that is why she fell in love with him. He does not have the academic aspirations that his girl friend has so he did not apply to any top universities in the country. And even if he did, he would not have been accepted. He was accepted at the local college where his girlfriend was also accepted. He wants her to attend the college with him. He is very serious about her and wants to marry her. In fact, he was thinking about proposing to her at the college graduation and getting married soon afterwards. He dreamt of marrying her and pursuing university studies together with his girlfriend as husband and wife with a loving home they create for themselves in their hometown city where their families are located. He has shared some of his dreams with her.

His girlfriend loves him, but has dreams of being a great writer someday. She knows that Williams College is an important step in fulfilling that dream. She knows that she has the talent and the gift to achieve her professional dream, and this dream is important to her. But she also loves him and can see a future with him. Ideally, she could continue the relationship long distance and pursue her professional dream. Her boyfriend does not like this idea. He can't bear to be apart from her. And he believes that he will lose her to someone else if she goes off to college. He has told her that if she goes off to college, thousands of miles away, to Williams College, he prefers to break up. She is undecided as what to do.

She shared her concerns with her father and described the situation to him. Although he likes her boyfriend, the father does not think that he is good enough for her. He honestly prefers that she finds someone else to date and marry. He thinks that Williams College will be a great opportunity for his daughter to meet the kind of guy that deserves her. Furthermore, the father wants his daughter to pursue her dreams, professionally. He has seen how she has spent sleepless nights studying and knows that she is serious about academics and her future. The father believes that his daughter has the potential to succeed as a great writer and Williams College is a step in the right direction. The father does not want to see his daughter hurt but feels that she will recover quickly from the break-up and will meet a wonderful guy at Williams.

The father, his daughter, and her boyfriend go to have ice cream at Dairy Queen with all this in the background. Throughout the dinner, the boyfriend is his good natured self and jokes around with the father and the daughter. They enjoy their company, but both realize that a decision has to be made about Williams College. The father is sure that it is the right step for his daughter. The daughter is still undecided but slightly leaning toward Williams College. The father knows this, but the boyfriend does not. They all have placed their orders. Soon, their desert comes. The daughter has ordered a strawberry ice cream sundae. The boyfriend has ordered a banana split. But instead of ordering ice cream, the father has ordered a piece of chocolate cake. There is a scoop of vanilla ice cream on the side.

As the waitress brings their deserts, the father says to the boyfriend, "I was always curious about one thing." The boy friend responds, "What is that, Mr. Jones?" The father asks the question, "Who is your favorite writer?" The boy friend tenses up because he sees what the father is trying to do. The boyfriend knows that the father means well but is resentfully aware that the father thinks that he is not good enough for his daughter. Not being so academic, he doesn't like to read. So, he could not think of any writers on the spot. Instead of dignifying the question with a serious answer, the boyfriend resorts to a joke and tries to brush off the question. The father has a laugh at the joke but gives his daughter a look. The daughter who wants to be a great writer is somewhat upset at the boyfriend's reply and understands the look that her father is giving her as a negative strike against her boyfriend.

Their deserts are placed before them. The daughter has the strawberry sundae. The boyfriend has the banana split. And the father has the chocolate cake with vanilla ice cream on the side. The father says, "Wow, your ice cream looks great. Maybe I should have ordered ice cream. But I do like my chocolate desert. It reminds me of my college days when I was dating your mother, Mrs. Jones, who wasn't Mrs. Jones, yet, at that time." The daughter smiles and looks at her father. She says politely, "Your chocolate cake looks really good, dad." The father smiles and says, "I think you are right. And I will have my chocolate cake!" And the father takes a bit out of his chocolate cake. The daughter looks at her father pensively.

What has happened? The father has used a key signifier. Can you identify the key signifier? The key signifier that the father has used is "I will have my chocolate cake." Can you see how this functions as a key signifier? As we recall, a key signifier recalls a collective memory or a community value and it triggers an action. Let us identity the dual triggering mechanism of the key signifier of "I will have my chocolate cake."

Let us begin with the question: What collective memory or community value does this key signifier recall? Most of you who are Americans may have guessed it by now. The collective memory that the key signifier recalls is the saying, "You can't have your cake and eat it, too." It's an American saying, so those who are not Americans may not be aware of the saying or know what it means.

In other words, if you are not American, you may not necessarily identify with the collective memory that is being recalled by the key signifier. This highlights the important fact of key signifiers. There has to be a shared collective memory. The collective memory can be a saying, a piece of literature, a movie, or some kind of cultural text or religious experience. Without participating in the collective memory, a key signifier will not work. Put it another way, you have to be a part of the in-group vis-à-vis collective memory in order to be impacted by the key signifier. Thus, a key signifier that works in the Korean-American context, like "1.5 generation," may not work in the context of a room full of French people.

Most Americans know the saying, "You can't have your cake and eat it, too." Thus, this is a part of the collective memory of Americans. It is this collective memory that the key signifier of "I will have my chocolate cake," uttered by the father recalls. Americans will participate in the recall of this collective memory. And the daughter, who is American, will participate in the recall of this collective memory as well.

We see the collective memory that the key signifier is soliciting. The next logical question is: What is the action sought by the key signifier? What action is the father intending to compel by using the key signifier of "I will have my chocolate cake"?

The father is trying to get her daughter to decide between the two choices: to stay with her boyfriend in her hometown and continue her relationship with him or to go to Williams College in search of her dream to be a great writer. It is obvious which choice her father desires her to choose. In fact, the father has intentionally used the key signifier to compel his daughter to decide for once and for all to go to Williams College, even if it means breaking up with her boyfriend who is sitting right next to her.

How do we know this? We know this from the content of the story. The father asks his daughter's boyfriend who his favorite author is. This is a kind of a set-up. The father is trying to set up an opposition between the boyfriend and the world of writing. And the father succeeds. But the father did not have to do much work in this regard, because the opposition was already there. It was his own daughter who described the situation as choosing between her boyfriend whom she loves and the college which could make her into a great writer. The dialectic was her dialectic, so the daughter did not need any convincing in that regard.

The content of the story reveals more about the fact that the father intentionally used the key signifier of "I will have my chocolate cake" to compel his daughter to choose Williams College over her boyfriend. The father deliberately orders a desert that is different from the desert of his daughter and her boyfriend. They order ice cream, and the father orders a cake. This is a form of objecting to the relationship between his daughter and her boyfriend. The father knew that his daughter and her boyfriend will order ice cream. In fact, they were in an ice cream place. People do not normally go to Dairy Queen to have cake or other kinds of non-ice cream desert.

Like most people in Dairy Queen, the father anticipated that his daughter and her boyfriend will order ice cream. Ordering a cake instead of an ice cream would have been an action that would have been contrary to the in-group experience in the context of Dairy Queen. In this action, the father is encouraging his daughter to go out of state to a college thousands of miles away. He is standing by her option to go to Williams College and standing against the in-group of people present.

Furthermore, the fact that the father explicitly points out the reality that he had chocolate cake with his wife during the days they dated in college is significant. It is a way for the father to tell his daughter that just as he met his wife in college, she too can meet her husband in college. She should not be afraid about leaving her boyfriend and going off to college without a boyfriend. She can meet a nice guy at Williams. Indeed, the fact that the father specifically mentions his dating in college in association with the chocolate cake that he ordered is a clear indicator of the intended effect of the key signifier, "I will have my chocolate cake." The father wanted his daughter to choose Williams College over her boyfriend.

Thus, we see how the key signifier of "I will have my chocolate cake" functions in a conversation context in a normal life setting. There are key signifiers employed all the time. We do so without thinking about it many times.

It is like using metaphor and simile. We use them all the time in our everyday conversation and speech, but we don't think about the fact that we are using them. In fact, ever since there was speech, literary devices of metaphor and simile were employed. This is clearly evident in written texts from the ancient world. Thousands of years before the literary devices of the metaphor and the simile were identified, people were using them in normal speech and conversation. Even today, people who do not know precisely what the literary devices of metaphor and simile are are using them in their common, everyday speech and conversations.

Likewise, the key signifier is being used every day by normal people. And writers are using the key signifier in their writing without being aware of the fact that they are employing this literary device. This is why this book is very important. This book coins and defines the literary device of the key signifier and describes its nature and function. After reading this book and digesting it, the literary critic will be able to identify key signifiers in literature and media.

Now, we can turn to the movies and examine the use of key signifiers in media. The movie that I have chosen to examine is *Hum Dil De Chuke Sanam* (1999) from India. The international English title of this movie is "Straight from the Heart." This movie is in Hindi with English subtitles. Besides being a great movie that is very entertaining to watch, this movie contains some significant key signifiers. Furthermore, I have purposely chosen a foreign film. This way we can see key signifiers operating in media as well as understand that the literary device of the key signifier can operate in non-western contexts and non-western media. Furthermore, because the movie involves a traditional Hindi family, it allows us an opportunity to examine key signifiers in a socio-religious tradition that may not be familiar with the majority of Americans and other westerners.

Since most Americans are not as familiar with Bollywood and Indian cinema, I will provide some background information that can be constructive to studying key signifiers in the Indian film. Let me start by introducing the actors.

The main star of the film is Aishwarya Rai, whose nickname is "The Queen of Bollywood." She is actually quite famous even in the American context, so some of the readers will have heard of her name or have seen her interviews in American TV. In 2005, Aishwarya Rai appeared in "60 Minutes," "David Letterman Show," and "Oprah Winfrey Show." She is most famous for her part in the critically acclaimed film, Sanjay Leela Bhansali's *Devdas* (2002), which was the most successful film in Bollywood history.

Devdas (2002) received international attention. It was the first Bollywood film to receive a special screening at Cannes Film Festival. Aishwarya Rai's part in the film along with her long history of talented acting brought her the great honor of being the first Indian actor to be a member of the jury at Cannes Film Festival in 2003. In 2004, Aishwarya Rai became the first Indian female to be immortalized as a wax figure at London's Madame Tussaud's Wax Museum.

Aishwarya Rai has come a long way from her roots in Mangalore, Karnataka, India, where she was born on November 1, 1973. For an architecture student who reluctantly entered the film industry after winning Miss Word 1994, she has made a mark in the history of cinema, and she seems to be going strong.

This comes to show that as unfamiliar as *Hum Dil De Chuke Sanam* (1999) may be to some Americans, it is a major film with internationally respected actors. Other main actors include Salman Khan and Ajay Devgan, who are respected actors in their own right. One interesting fact is that this movie was what started the relationship between Salman Khan and Aishwarya Rai. It was the most publicized romance in the history of Indian Cinema. Interestingly enough, the relationship that Aishwarya Rai's character Nadini could not consummate with Salman Khan's character, Sameer Rafilini, in the movie was consummated in the real life of the actors who played their roles in the movie.

Hum Dil De Chuke Sanam (1999) was a film by Sanjay Leela Bhansali, who also made the film *Devdas* (2002). In a sense, this movie can be seen as a tribute to traditional Indian way of life and the Hindu religion. The movie begins with Sameer Rafilini (Salman Khan) coming into the traditional Hindu home of Pundit Darbar (Vikram Gokhale), who is a famous singer and music teacher. Sameer Rafilini seeks to study music with Pundit Barbar and is accepted as his student. Pundit Darbar tells his daughter Nadini (Aishwarya Rai) to clear her room for Sameer Rafilini. Nadini resents this request, but obeys her father, like a good Hindi daughter is expected to. We see from the beginning of the film that this tension will spark an intense love between Nadini and Sameer.

Sameer is half Indian and half Italian, so he can speak both languages fluently. His home is in Italy. Although half Indian, his mannerisms are distinctively non-Indian. Sameer clearly stands out as an outsider, and this sparks Nadini's interest even further. Sameer is jocular and not serious in any way. In a sense, he is stereotypically western as perceived by Asians. In this stereotypically western way, Sameer begins to try to win the heart of Nadini, and he succeeds. After Sameer has won her heart, Nadini grows frustrated because Sameer continues to be not serious in her mind. She tells him that if he is not serious then she will be taken from under his eyes. Some other guy will ask for her hand in marriage, and she will end up marrying him. This turns out to be a self-fulfilling prophecy. Despite Nadini's efforts to get Sameer to act seriously about his love for her, which means to have him ask her father for her hand in marriage, Sameer does not follow the traditional Indian ways.

The audience is left to wonder if it is because Sameer is superficial and maybe not genuine about his love for Nadini. This would reinforce the stereotype that westerners are superficial and not genuine. And Sameer's constant joking around seems to reinforce this notion. Furthermore, when Nadini's father, Pundit Darbar, asks Sameer to leave his home, Sameer just leaves without putting up a fight. This makes the audience wonder if Sameer truly loved her in the first place.

In Sameer's defense, Pundit Darbar requests that the payment (guru-dakshina) for music instructions be the promise that Sameer leave and leave his daughter alone. Sameer's walking through the desert after leaving Pundit

Darbar's house seems to confirm the possibility that he may actually be quite poor and could not negotiate a payment of another kind. Still, the audience is left to wonder why Sameer did not take the opportunity to testify to his love for Nadini to her father. Why didn't he even try?

The guy that Nadini marries is completely the opposite of Sameer. Vanraj is a traditional Indian, who comes from a respectable Hindi family. He is self-composed and seems to know what he wants out of life. He does not engage in juvenile dating rituals with Nadini but approaches her with seriousness that testifies to his serious love for her. Vanraj does everything right. He asks for Nadini's hand in marriage through traditional Indian means. And even after they are married, Vanraj treats Nadini with respect and honor.

Even when Nadini forbids her husband to touch her or make love to her, Vanraj is patient and supportive of his wife. When Vanraj finds out that Nadini is in love with another man, Vanraj shows himself to be a man by getting angry and expressing his discontent in masculine ways. Thus, the audience is left to understand that Vanraj's patience and good treatment of Nadini did not come out of some kind of effeminate fear but rather out of deep-seated contentment of a man who is in harmony with his religion, family, and self.

After expressing the righteous anger of the husband, Vanraj shows his kindness and generosity in promising to unite Nadini to her lover, Sameer. Together, Nadini and Vanraj fly to Italy in search of Sameer. In the process of searching for him, they are robbed by a western couple and in the struggle Nadini is shot. Through it all, Vanraj is a faithful and supportive husband who understands and executes his duty as a husband as demanded by traditional Hindu ways. Thus, Vanraj is the epitome of the respectable and honorable Hindu male.

Finally, Nadini gets well and meets Sameer. Sameer has not changed at all. He is still the not serious, flippant, stereotypical westerner who doesn't think seriously about the troubles that Nadini went through. He seems self-absorbed in himself. Nadini begins to see Sameer for who he is, and ends up falling in love with Vanraj. In fact, Nadini chooses Vanraj over Sameer, when the situation was favorable to choose Sameer over Nadini.

This is symbolic of triumph of traditional Indian ways over stereotypically western superficiality. This was triumph of Hinduism and Hindu values over secularized Christianity and the superficiality that western Christians seemed to represent. This was triumph of true love based on duty and obligation over senseless talk and selfish romance. As is evident, *Hum Dil De Chuke Sanam* (1999) is a tribute to Hinduism and traditional Indian lifestyle.

This is an important thing to remember when looking for the literary device of the key signifier in *Hum Dil De Chuke Sanam* (1999). What are the key signifiers? I will focus on one central key signifier – namely, the left hand. We can use language to describe the key signifier, but in the movie, the key signifier of the left hand is visual. There are two major scenes where this key signifier is used, and I will describe them. And then we can discuss how the left hand functions as a key signifier.

The first attestation of the key signifier of the left hand occurs in a wedding banquet, where Nadini gives a dance performance for the guests present. As a part of her dance routine, she throws a yellow ball into the audience. She throws the yellow ball with her left hand in the direction of Vanraj. Vanraj catches the ball and hides it in his right hand. The idea is that since Vanraj caught the ball, Nadini will now go to reclaim the ball. Vanraj will hide the ball in one of his two hands, and Nadini has to guess which hand has the hidden ball.

Although Vanraj hides the ball in his right hand, his sister persuades him to hide the ball in his left hand. Vanraj complies and changes hands and hides the ball in his left hand. Nadini approaches Vanraj. This is the first time she sees him in the movie. Nadini looks at Vanraj and points to his right hand. Vanraj reveals his right hand, and it is empty. Thus, Nadini points to the left hand. When Vanraj opens his left hand, there is the yellow ball.

This episode took place after Vanraj's sister had commented to Vanraj that he should find a nice woman to marry. Since this was the prelude to the scene, the audience is left to understand that the meeting of Nadini and Vanraj would result in marriage. And it does. Soon after the meeting, Vanraj contacts Nadini's parents to ask her hand in marriage.

The second attestation of the key signifier of the left hand occurs at the end of the movie in the final scene. After a long search in Italy, Nadini finally found Sameer. As Nadini goes to meet Sameer, Vanraj leaves his wife and goes away. Nadini talks with Sameer and realizes that she is no longer in love with Sameer, that it was an infatuation. She is in love with her husband, Vanraj. So, Nadini rushes out to find Vanraj. Finally, Nadini catches up to Vanraj. In the brief encounter, Vanraj realizes that Nadini loves him and has chosen him. Nadini stretches out her two hands for Vanraj to choose. This is reminiscent of the scene containing the first attestation of the key signifier of the left hand – namely, in the context of Nadini's dance at a wedding party.

Vanraj chooses the left hand. When Nadini opens her left hand, inside is her marriage necklace. She puts the necklace back on herself in a symbolic gesture testifying to her desire and will be his wife out of her own decision. And it is on this happy note, the movie ends.

Now that we know where the key signifier of the left hand occurs, we can ask the question of how it is a key signifier. As we know, the key signifier has a dual trigger mechanism; it recalls a collective memory or community value and triggers an action by the audience as a result.

First, let us look at the community value or the collective memory that the key signifier is recalling. The left hand in the Indian cultural context is seen as impure or dirty. This is the result of the historical use of the left hand. Whereas the right hand was used for eating, historically, the left hand was used like toilet paper. In the absence of paper, this was practical, and water could be used to purify the hand. But since historically, there were distinctive functions for the right hand and for the left hand, they took on symbolic significance and cultural bans. Thus, it was culturally forbidden to shake hands with your left hand. It was seen as symbolically impure.

The key signifier of the left hand, thus, recalls this collective memory of the left hand as impure. How does this relate to the two attestations of the key signifier? The first attestation of the key signifier of the left hand was the first meeting of Vanraj and Nadini. It was the prelude to their marriage. The key signifier should be viewed in this light. When Vanraj catches the ball thrown by Nadini, he hides the ball first in his right hand. This indicates that Vanraj wants to give Nadini his pure hand, representing his pure desire to marry her. But in the encounter representing the first greeting, Vanraj changes hands and hides the ball in the left hand. But he did not do this out of his own will but because his sister encouraged him to do it. It indicates that what he did not see, his sister saw. Nadini should not be given an honorable greeting, but a dishonorable one. This episode proves to be prophetic in that Vanraj finds out that Nadini's intentions were not pure in marrying him. Nadini married him while loving another man.

The fact that his sister encourages Vanraj to change from right hand to left hand was an indication that Nadini was not a good choice for marriage. There was something impure hidden, to be revealed at a later date. The fact that Nadini threw the ball to Vanraj with her left hand was a bad omen. Why would she initiate her greeting with the impure left hand and not with the pure right hand? Nadini approached Vanrai with impure motives, but Vanraj wanted to offer her his right hand, so he originally hid the ball in his right hand.

When Nadini approached Vanraj, she pointed to the right hand. It was a typical way of greeting someone in India, to extend greeting to the right hand. Vanraj opened his right hand, and it was empty. Nadini, then, pointed to the left hand. Vanraj opened his left hand, and the ball was revealed. Nadini took the ball from Vanraj and continued with her dance. The symbolic exchange has taken place between Nadini and Vanraj, but the greeting with left hands was a bad omen. Their relationship would begin on impurity, rather than purity.

The key signifier of the left hand recalled the collective memory of the impurity of the left hand. Left hand was associated with all that was bad or dirty or lacking virtue. The right hand was the clean hand that brought food to the body, symbolizing purity, goodness, and righteousness. The collective memory of the left hand in the wedding banquet scene informed the audience about the inauspicious nature of the meeting.

This was confirmed when Vanraj and Nadini were married. Nadini married Vanraj, still loving another man. Although she never had sex with him, Nadini had given her heart to Sameer. She should have been honest with Vanraj, and let him know before the marriage. But Nadini did not. Vanraj tells Nadini that he can handle anything, except lies. Thus, for Vanraq, Nadini committed the greatest wrong against him that a person could commit. It was like Nadini wanted a relationship with Sameer, but when that came up empty, Nadini settled for Vanraj. Sameer represented the right hand that was empty, and Vanraj represented the left hand that had the ball, but which was the second choice.

We see that the key signifier of the left hand functions as a key signifier should – recalling a collective memory typically associated with the key signifier. Even the narrative of the movie supports this recall of the key signifier. The second attestation of the key signifier of the left hand also functions as a key signifier should.

In the final scene, we find Vanraj and Nadini again in a situation not dissimilar to the first attestation of the key signifier of the left hand where choosing of one hand over the other is involved. But this time, it is not Nadini choosing one of Vanraj's hands. The roles are inverted. Now, it was Vanraj choosing one of Nadini's hands. Out of nowhere, Nadini pulls out her both of her hands for Vanraj to choose. This recalls the time when Vanraj and Nadini met for the first time at the wedding banquet. Vanraj knows what is expected of him. He is to choose one of the hands.

Vanraj chooses Nadini's left hand. Unlike Nadini, who instinctively went for the right hand – a typical Indian response given the symbols attached to the left hand and the function of the right hand – Vanraj chooses Nadini's left hand as his first choice. This would not have been a typical Indian choice. And we know that Vanraj is not inclined to choose the left hand because Vanraj chose his right hand to hide the ball at the wedding banquet. Choosing of Nadini's left hand as his hand of choice was out of the ordinary. And that is where the key signifier of the left hand functions effectively. The audience watching the movie knows what the left hand symbolizes if they are of Indian descent, familiar with Indian traditional ways.

Vanraj's choosing the left hand of Nadini is quite revealing. It is symbolic of Vanraj's choice of Nadini and marriage to her. Nadini was Vanraj's first choice to be his wife. Vanraj was honorable and upright in pursuing Nadini as his wife. Although he was honorable, Nadini was not. Without knowing it, Vanraj was choosing someone who was dishnorable and impure in her motives – all the things associated with the collective memory that the left hand recalled. Thus, Vanraj choosing Nadini's left hand as his first choice describes his relationship to Nadini. He has chosen someone who was not only impure in her motives, but also brings him bad luck and dishonor. Vanraj has chosen the left hand over the right hand in choosing Nadini. And it was his first choice.

When Nadini opens up her left hand, there is something inside. It's not the yellow ball of the wedding. Rather, it is the necklace which symbolizes her marriage to Vanraj. The fact that she held this necklace in her left hand can be seen as sacrilegious. How could she commit something so sacred as the wedding necklace to her impure left hand? She should have held it with her pure right hand. The fact that Nadini chose to hide the marriage necklace in her left hand shows the attitude with which Nadini treated the sacred institution of marriage. Nadini had treated her marriage to Vanraj like something out of the gutter.

The scene immediately before the final scene testifies to this. Nadini meets Sameer on his big night. It is the first time that they met after Sameer left India. This was made possible because Vanraj in his good karma aided Nadini in finding her "true love." Vanraj went through a lot to bring Nadini to Italy to find her lover. On a personal level, it was humiliating to bring his wife to find her lover. This humiliation is brought out when Vanraj introduces his wife to Italians in the movie. He struggles because he doesn't know what to call her. She is his wife, but they were in this awkward situation.

But the humiliation was not only on a psychological level. His father chastised him in the movie for what Vanraj decided to do. Vanraj in maintaining a positive karma was misunderstood by his own family members. They indicated to him that he had been dishonored. And in Vanraj's dishonor, his family felt dishonor and shame.

But still, Vanraj went through the greatest difficult possibility to find Sameer for Nadini. Throughout their time in Italy, Nadini was fixated on Sameer and eagerly (and visibly) looked for Sameer. Vanraj was like an appendage fixed peripherally to the search for Sameer. And Nadini made Vanraj feel bad constantly. Nadini kept Vanraj at a physical distance and disdained his touch. When Nadini showed something resembling affection to Vanraj, it seemed forced. The taxi scene in Italy illustrates this. Nadini gets into the taxi and then looks at Vanraj. After throwing him a look of pity, she slowly moves to the other side of the back seat of the taxi to make room for Vanraj. Vanraj understands the innate insult of the situation and refuses to get in the back seat of the taxi with her. This illustrated that Vanraj understood the whole humiliating situation. He also understood that Nadini did not really care for him. Despite the humiliation and his understanding of the situation, Vanraj decided to help. This clearly testifies to Vanraj's honor and virtue. He deserves the right hand and not the left hand.

When the search is complete and Sameer is found, Nadini discards Vanraj and rushes off to Sameer. She has every intention of joining Sameer and leaving Vanraj. But the meeting of Sameer and Nadini again proves that it was like choosing the empty right hand. Sameer is not serious about her and treats her like he always did. Sameer had left Nadini and did not fight for her when he had the chance to with her father. Nadini had wept bitterly about this separation. She, in fact, had attempted suicide over her love for Sameer. What did Sameer do? He lived his life like nothing had happened – as if Nadini was a bleep in his life. The scene where Sameer and Nadini meet in Italy confirms this.

Like the time when Sameer was in India, it is Nadini who does all the work. Nadini had told Sameer to be serious about his love and encouraged him to ask for her hand in marriage to her father. Sameer ignored this. It was Nadini who tried to make their relationship work and lead it to the honorable conclusion of marriage. But Sameer abandoned his obligation to her and his role in the whole marriage process. Sameer did not pursue an honorable end. The second meeting – the meeting in Italy – was reminiscent of the relationship of Sameer and Nadini in India. Sameer did not try at all to find Nadini or bring about an honorable end. Sameer could have easily located Nadini because he knew where Nadini lived. He could have tried to talk to Nadini's father because he knew him and knew where he was. Sameer just does not try.

In contrast, Nadini did not know where Sameer was. She only knew that he was from Italy. It was Nadini who tries to find him. It was Nadini who tries to make their love work. And Vanraj helps her because he believes that there is something noble about true love. Furthermore, Vanraj wants to have an honorable conclusion in his relationship to Nadini. He truly loves her, but he does not want to love her if she does not love him and wants to give her heart to someone else.

The meeting between Nadini and Sameer happened because of a great sacrifice on Nadini's part – and also on the part of her husband, Vanraj. But

Sameer does not seem to appreciate the difficulty. Sameer is self-absorbed about his own situation. He does not ask about the difficulty involved in Nadini finding him out in Italy. Sameer assumes that it is a simple matter, not involving any difficult struggle. Nadini realizes at this meeting in Italy that Sameer does not really love her. She realizes that the love of Vanraj was the true love. Love demanded personal sacrifice. And clearly, Vanraj made great personal sacrifices for Nadini. Vanraj was the epitome of the virtuous Hindu man, who is self-giving and full of good karma. In fact, Vanraj embodied the positive symbol of the right hand. But Nadini decided to choose Sameer as the right hand. It was no surprise that she came up empty, like the first time.

Realizing that Sameer did not truly love her and realizing that she was in infatuation and not in true love, she turns to the person who had shown her true love – namely, Vanraj. She rushes out to meet him. But like the first time, she rushed to Vanraj after she chose what she perceived as the right hand, which came up empty. Vanraj was relegated to the second choice, left hand, yet again.

But when Nadini and Vanraj meet, she still does not dignify her marriage by placing the marriage necklace in her right hand. Nadini has thoroughly desecrated the marriage and dishonored Vanraj according to the Hindu tradition. Vanraj knows this. Thus, instead of instinctively going for the right hand, which would have been normative and in keeping with his personal preference, Vanraj goes for Nadini's left hand. Even though Vanraj knew that she acted like someone out of the gutter, he will choose her because she was his wife. It is no accident that the left hand revealed the emblem of their marriage. Their marriage has been dragged through the dirt, but still the institution of the marriage was sacred and Vanraj will practice his Hindu piety and practice forgiveness for the sake of sacred vows.

Thus, we see the key signifier of the left hand operating strongly in the movie, *Hum Dil De Chuke Sanam* (1999). This key signifier ties the whole plot of the movie together. And it is this key signifier that not only provides the climax of the film leading to the departure of Sameer and the marriage between Vanraj and Nadini, but also ends the movie.

We have seen how the key signifier of the left hand operates in recalling the collective memory associated with the left hand. Now, we can ask the question about what action the key signifier of the left hand prompts in the audience.

The key signifier of the left hand prompts the Indian audience to traditional Hindu piety in the context of the movie. Before examining how this works, I would like to identify the key signifier of the left hand as a hybrid key signifier in that it is a hybrid of the generated key signifier and the received key signifier. As we recall, we talked about how "Beloved" was a generated key signifier in the context of Toni Morrison's novel. It is a generated key signifier because the key signifier was created by Toni Morrison herself in the context of her novel. Toni Morrison did not create collective memory. It was already there. We identified that collective memory as slavery. But it was Toni Morrison who created the key signifier of "Beloved" and connected it with the collective memory of slavery.

In contrast, received key signifiers are those words or phrases that already functions as key signifiers in a culture or among the in-group. One of the examples we gave as a received key signifier is "up to half the kingdom." By the time that this key signifier was used in the Markan pericope, it had been in existence for centuries. The key signifier was a vital part of the book of Esther as well as the ritualistic celebration of Purim. When the author of the Markan pericope used the key signifier of "up to half the kingdom," he did not need to explain it or create a narrative support for it because it was fully operational as a received key signifier. Perhaps, we can talk about the key signifier being created at the composition of the book of Esther, but we certainly cannot talk about the "creation" of the key signifier in the context of the Gospel of Mark. It was a received key signifier by the time of Jesus of Nazareth in the Jewish context.

When we talk about a hybrid key signifier, we are talking about a key signifier that combines elements of a received key signifier and of generated key signifier. The most usual way a hybrid key signifier works is that the key signifier is a received key signifier, but further meaning, content, or contextual understanding is added onto the received key signifier. In other words, the received key signifier takes on elaboration and fine-tuning. This is what happened with the key signifier of the left hand.

The key signifier of the left hand already was functioning as a received key signifier in the Indian context. It recalled the collective memory of all that was dishonorable, impure, or trash-like. It recalled the collective memory of what the left hand was traditionally used for; thus, it recalled human excrement. In this cultural context, shaking hands with the left hand or extending the left hand would have been a great insult because of the key signifier of the left hand that recalled the collective memory of the Indian people.

Thus, we cannot talk about the key signifier as created or generated in the movie. It was a received key signifier. However, the movie fashioned the key signifier consciously to give a more specific meaning and explanation to the general collective memory that the key signifier recalled. Plot, symbolism, and characterization were used to give more specific details to what actually was dishonorable, dirty, impure, and unfair – all the elements associated in the collective memory with the left hand. I have shown above how this was done in the context of the movie. It was this conscious effort to arrive at a specificity of the reference that makes the key signifier of the left hand a hybrid key signifier in *Hum Dil De Chuke Sanam* (1999). The hybrid key signifier particularizes the general use of the received key signifier of the left hand.

Now that we have discussed the nature of the key signifier of the left hand in the context of the movie which we are examining, we can go on to our discussion of what action this hybrid key signifier triggers in the audience. As mentioned before, the action that this hybrid key signifier of the left hand in the movie triggers is a piety toward traditional Hindu ways.

Let us examine the two attestations in the movie of the hybrid key signifier of the left hand with attention to the traditional Hindu piety that the key signifier is trying to actuate. In the first scene, Nadini chooses the left hand only after choosing the right hand, which turned up empty. How does the hybrid key signifier of the left hand in this scene prompt the audience toward traditional Hindu piety? This scene in the context of the whole movie causes Indian audiences to see the dangers of deviating from traditional Indian ways. For instance, although it seemed "fun" for Nadini to engage in a western style of flirting and dating, it turned up empty like the right hand Nadini chose first. Her emotions were toyed with, and Sameer was not serious about love. The message is that if you date around or flirt around like in the west, you will turn up empty. You will suffer because of your love but your love will not be consummated in marriage.

The audience, therefore, is encouraged to guard against western influences in terms of dating. This idea is supported by the scene where Pundit Darbar, Nadini's father, discovers that Nadini has been carrying on with Sameer. When one under his *pater familias* authority accuses Nadini of having an affair with a boy in disregard for traditional Hindu ways, Pundit dismisses the suggestion right away. Pundit Darbar, who is a famous singer and makes his living through singing, impulsively swears that he will never sing again if it is true that Nadini is flirting around with a boy against the dictates of traditional Hinduism. Pundit says that Nadini is as pure as the songs that he sings. Pundit believed his daughter to be the embodiment of the purity of Hinduism.

When Pundit Darbar, Nadini's father, discovers that Nadini, in fact, had been flirting around with Sameer and was having a love affair – although a non-sexual one – he is devastated. Nadini had gone against traditional Hindu ways. Thus, he gives up singing altogether like he promised in his oath. Thus, we see that the world is deprived of the wonderful voice and singing of Pundit Darbar. It is like a bad karma created by Nadini's violation of the purity of Hinduism, and this bad karma ended up depriving everyone in the world of the divine gift of Pundit Darbar's songs.

Thus, Nadini's pursuit of happiness through Sameer against the Hindu ways opened the Pandora's Box. Not only did she fall in love and give her emotion and self away to someone who was not serious about her, she destroyed her father's career and his ability to make a living. Going against traditional Hindu ways has consequences – real negative consequences that affect not only you but also those whom you love.

This is fundamentally a part of the narrative of the movie, and the hybrid key signifier of the left hand is integrally tied to this idea. Why did Nadini choose Sameer? Why did Nadini choose Sameer as her right hand? Why did Nadini go against traditional Hindu ways? Why did Nadini relegate traditional Hindu marriage to a place of the left hand, a place of dishonor and filth? The audience, through a vicarious participation in the movie experience, are to ask themselves such questions. Furthermore, they are compelled to question of themselves. Is it worth it to deviate from traditional Hindu ways and bring dishonor to my father? And it may not be only dishonor that I bring upon my father. There may be more dire consequences like my anti-Hindu actions hurting my father's social standing or even his ability to make a living. Thus, the audience is compelled through the hybrid key signifier of the left hand in the context of the movie to gravitate toward traditional Hindu religion and its instructions regarding marriage and dating. The message is: Do not relegate marriage (represented by the yellow ball) to a place of dishonor (represented by the left hand) by acting against traditional Hindu ways. It will cost you and those you love.

Like the first attestation of the hybrid key signifier of the left hand, the second attestation in the final scene of the movie also prompts the audience toward traditional Hindu piety. This is clear in the context of the movie. Nadini had travelled the world for her true love, and as romantic as this sounds, all the effort and energy spent ended up with nothing. What she thought of as true love was merely infatuation. All that Nadini ended up doing was dragging her marriage through the mud. It was in the left hand of Nadini that her marriage necklace was placed by her own hand. Nadini had placed the sacred institution of the marriage in the toilet because she refused to honor traditional Hindu teaching about marriage and pursued what she thought was true love. Nadini realizes that true love is devotion and duty as outlined in Hinduism – which her husband Vanraj embodied and which Sameer did not even know.

The hybrid key signifier of the left hand in the final scene – which contained the marriage necklace – compels the Hindu audience toward traditional Hindu piety, particularly in regards to the sacred Hindu institution of marriage and the duties of the husband and wife. Love is not a fleeting emotion, it is a concerted effort borne out of duty and self-sacrifice as traditional Hinduism teaches. Searching for "true love" is useless and will only end up in heartache and desecration of the traditional Hindu values regarding marriage. The Hindu audience should follow traditional Indian ways and work within the Hindu system to find true love rather than chasing after an infatuation. There is virtue in Hinduism and its teaching about love and marriage duty. This is the message that the audience is compelled to take with them as the result of the hybrid key signifier of the left hand in the final scene of the movie. As they leave the movie theater, the youngsters who are not yet married are encouraged to gravitate toward traditional Hindu ways and its teaching regarding love and marriage, and not to chase after an infatuation. Those who are married in the audience are discouraged to a misguided notion of romance and true love that could drag their marriage through human excrement. Even if they disrespect the sacred institution of marriage – even with their husband's help – the infatuation which they thought as love would end up only in heartbreak and emptiness. All of that for what? Thus, as the Hindu audience leaves the movie theatre, they are compelled toward greater

Hindu piety, particularly in regards to marriage and dating. This is the final trigger mechanism of the hybrid key signifier of the left hand as developed and used in the movie, *Hum Dil De Chuke Sanam* (1999), which is translated in English by the movie makers as "Straight from the Heart."

In this chapter, we have discussed how the literary device of the key signifier can be used in media. And we have focused on the media of movies and used *Hum Dil De Chuke Sanam* (1999), a famous Bollywood movie from India, to understand the workings of the literary device of the key signifier. In the process, we came to understand how a key signifier can be developed based on a received key signifier. We called this key signifier – which combines elements belonging to the received key signifier and the generated key signifier – a "hybrid key signifier."

This chapter also discussed the use of key signifiers in speech and normal, everyday conversation, as a way to show that key signifiers, like any other literary device like the metaphor or simile, can be employed in written text as well as any kind of spoken text, including various media channels, like the movies or TV shows. Understanding the nature and function of key signifiers in media can help a movie maker or other participants in media to create artistic masterpiece that speaks to the collective memory of a people. We hope that this book will help some movie makers to become brilliant in this regard.

Conclusion

In this book, we have looked together at the nature and function of the literary device of the key signifier – a literary device which I coined formally at the Apocrypha and Pseudepigrapha Section of the 2005 International Meeting of the Society of Biblical Literature in Singapore (June 26 – July 1, 2005). Although it had been formally coined in the context of an international academic conference in 2005, I have been working on the literary device of the key signifier for several years. Thus, various academics around the world are aware of my work on the key signifier from before 2005. I have also used the term in passing in various academic papers I have delivered at international conferences before the year 2005, although my focused presentation on the literary device of the key signifier in Singapore in 2005 represents the formal coining of the literary device in an academic setting. This book is the first comprehensive book on the literary device of the key signifier and will function for many years as the reference book for understanding the literary device of the key signifier. As a reference work, there is a generalizing tendency in the book, which is characteristic of most reference guides. However, I have begun to write a more indepth monograph on the function of the key signifier as used in Biblical literature. This would not be a reference work, but rather an application book dependent on this reference book. This book will see the light of publication in a few years' time. I do hope that there will be many articles and books using this reference book to apply the study of the literary device of the key signifier in particular literature, movies, and mass media. Hopefully, by time my "application" monograph is published, there will

154

be several monographs written by various scholars in diverse fields, as film, poetry, American literature, Chinese poetry, and the like.

We have discussed the literary device of the key signifier at length, and we have covered a lot of issues involved with the nature and function of the literary device of the key signifier. Let us briefly recap what we have discussed in this conclusion. As we recall, the definition of the literary device of the key signifier that I presented at the International Meeting of the Society of Biblical Literature in Singapore in 2005 was: "A key signifier is defined as a term or phrase that triggers a collective memory or a community value that is over-arching and all-encompassing. A key signifier functions aggressively in the literary context to spur audience to action." We have used this definition for this book.

We have summarized the definition in terms of dual (or double) triggering mechanism. On the one hand the key signifier triggers collective memory or community value. On the other hand, the key signifier triggers an action. The second trigger is dependent on the first trigger. Using this as a guide, we have examined the identity and function of the key signifier in various literary contexts, such as the Bible, the Apocrypha and the Pseudepigrapha, African-American literature, Chinese poetry, and the media (movies).

We have explained that the literary device of the key signifier can be identified not only in written literature, such as poetry and prose, but also in spoken speech, such as public speech or a normal, everyday conversation. We have also explained that key signifiers can be used in various mass media channels, such as movies, TV shows, and the news. In a sense, therefore, the key signifier can be identified wherever there is any form of communication.

We have also identified, described, and examined various types of key signifiers. These are the various types of key signifiers we have identified in this book: received key signifier, generated key signifier, hybrid key signifier, and intercultural key signifier. These are different types of key signifiers but they all fall under the general definition of the key signifier formally coined in Singapore in 2005.

Received key signifiers are key signifiers that already exist in the community of in-group members. Received key signifiers were formed as key signifiers some time in the distant past. Examples of received key signifiers include "up to half my kingdom" found in the Gospel of Mark 6:14-29 and "forever" in Psalms of Solomon 11. We have pointed out that the key signifier of "up to half my kingdom" is a received key signifier from the book of Esther and the Purim tradition. And we have explained that the key signifier of "forever" in Psalms of Solomon 11 is a received key signifier from Genesis 17 and the Abrahamic covenant tradition.

Generated key signifiers are key signifiers that are created by a writer or a movie producer – in fact, in any kind of communication. Generated key signifiers attach themselves artificially to collective memory or community value already extant in the community of in-group members. But for the link to be effective, there has to be narrative context that allows the connection to be made. Toni Morrison's novel, *Beloved*, is effective in generating the key signifier of "Beloved" that recall the collective memory of African-American slavery. Whether she fully appreciates it or not, Toni Morrison is a master of generated key signifiers as her other novels also show.

Hybrid key signifiers are key signifiers that combine the attributes of the received key signifier and the generated key signifier. Typically, hybrid key signifiers take received key signifiers and fine-tune them or add more specific meaning and content to them. We have presented the key signifier of the left hand in the Bollywood movie *Hum Dil De Chuke Sanam* as a good example of the hybrid key signifier. In the movie, the received key signifier of the left hand develops more specific content based on the narrative of the film, thereby adding generated elements to the received key signifier.

Intercultural key signifiers are key signifiers that are based on an experience of another people. The collective memory is embedded in the in-group, but based on the experiences of those who do not belong to the in-group. Ai Qing's poem, "Mao Zedong" from China, provided many ample examples of intercultural key signifiers. Ai Qing builds on the Chinese collective memory about Hitler and Nazism for his intercultural key signifiers in the poem.

All these types of key signifiers can be seen as belonging to a specific subgroup of key signifiers. However, they all have the dual triggering function. On the one hand they trigger the collective memory or community value of the in-group, and on the other hand, they compel the in-group members to action. Without this dual layered triggering function, a word or phrase would not be a key signifier.

I hope that reading this book has helped you understand what a key signifier is. I hope that this book has equipped you with the intellectual tools to identify and explain key signifiers in literature and media. Because key signifiers are a complex literary device, which opens the semantic and experiential world imbedded in a people's world and triggers the people toward a concrete action, they can open up the world of a people or of literature in ways simple literary devices like simile and metaphor cannot. However, because of the complexity of the literary device, more interdisciplinary study is need to understand the literary device and its function in the socio-historical context of a people hearing or reading a particular literature or watching a particular movie. In a sense, therefore, the literary device is a tribute to the growing trend and attempt in the humanities and social sciences to combine various diverse disciplines to understand better the human experience and the world which we inhabit. It is my sincerest hope that this book will contribute to the advancement of knowledge in humanistic disciplines and in the world of literature and the arts.

Bibliography

Abrahams, I. *Studies in Pharisaism and the Gospels.* New York: Ktav Publishing House, Inc., 1967.

Adams, Romanzo. *Interracial Marriage in Hawaii.* Montclair: Patterson Smith, 1937.

Ai, Qing. *Selected Poems.* Translated by Eugene Chen Eoyang, Peng Wenland, and Marilyn Chin. Beijing: Foreign Language Press, 1982.

Bailey, Randall C., and Jacquelyn Grant (Editors). *The Recovery of Black Presence: An Interdisciplinary Exploration* (Essays in Honor of Dr. Charles B. Copher). Nashville: Abingdon Press, 1995.

Barth, Gerhard. *Die Taufe in frühchristlicher Zeit.* Neukirchen-Vluyn: Neukirchener Verlag, 1981.

Bock, Emil. *Caesars and Apostles: Hellenism, Rome and Judaism.* Translated by Maria St. Goar. Edinburgh: Floris Books, 1998.

Bréhier, Émile. *Les Idées Philosophique et Religieuses de Philon d'Alexandrie.* Paris: Libraire Philosophique J. Vrin, 1950.

Bruce, F. F. *New Testament History.* New York: Doubleday, 1969.

Buchanan, George Wesley. *The Consequences of the Covenant.* Leiden: E. J. Brill, 1970.

Charles, R. H (Editor). *The Apocrypha and Pseudepigrapha of the Old Testament in English: With Introductions and Critical and Explanatory Notes to the Several Books.* Oxford: The Clarendon Press, 1913

Charlesworth, James H. *The Old Testament Psudepigrapha.* Garden City: Doubleday, 1923. (In 2 Voumes)

158

Che, Sunny. *Forever Alien: A Korean Memoir, 1930-1951*. Jefferson: McFarland & Company, Inc., Publishers, 2000.

Choi, Jai-Keun. *The Origin of the Roman Catholic Church in Korea: An Examination of Popular and Governmental Responses to Catholic Missions in the Late Chosôn Dynasty*. Cheltenham: The Hermit Kingdom Press, 2006.

Choy, Bong-Youn. *Koreans in America*. Chicago: Nelsen Hall, 1979.

De Vaux, Roland. *The Early History of Israel: To the Exodus and Covenant of Sinai*. Translated by David Smith. London: Darton, Longman & Todd, 1978.

Edwards, Chon S. *I Am Also A Daughter of Korea*. Seoul: Mi-Rae-Mun-Wha-Sa, 1988. [in Korean]

Everson, Susan Corey. "Toni Morrison's *Tar Baby*: A Resource for Feminist Theology." *Journal of Feminist Studies in Religion*. Vol. 5 No. 2 (Fall, 1989), pp. 65-78.

Fassberg, Steven E., and Avi Hurvitz (Editors). *Biblical Hebrew in Its Northwest Semitic Setting: Typological and Historical Perspectives*. Jerusalem: Hebrew University Magnes Press, 2006.

Felder, Cain Hope (Editor). *Stony the Road We Tread*. Minneapolis: Fortress, 1991.

Ferguson, Everett. *Backgrounds of Early Christianity*. Grand Rapids: William B. Eerdmans Publishing Company, 1987.

Fokkelman, J. P. *Narrative Art in Genesis: Specimens of Stylistic and Structural Analysis*. Assen: Van Gorcum, 1975.

Garbini, G. *History and Ideology in Ancient Israel*. London: 1988.

Ginsberg, Louis. *An Unknown Jewish Sect*. New York: The Jewish Theological Seminary of America, 1976.

Grewal, Gurleen. *Circles of Sorrow, Lines of Struggle*. Baton Rouge: Louisiana State University Press, 1998.

Griesinger, Emily. "Why Baby Suggs, Holy, Quit Preaching the Word: Redemption and Holiness in Toni Morrison's *Beloved.*" *Christianity and Literature.* Vol. 50 No. 4 (Summer 2001), pp. 689-702.

Gross, Seymour L., and John Edward Hardy (Editors). *Images of the Negro in American Literature.* Chicago: The University of Chicago Press, 1966.

Hamilton, V. P. *The Book of Genesis 1-17.* Grand Rapids: Eerdmans, 1990.

Harding, Wendy, and Jacky Martin. *A World of Difference: An Inter-Cultural Study of Toni Morrison's Novels.* Westport: Greenwood Press, 1994.

Holm-Nielsen, Svend. *Hodayot: Psalms from Qumran.* Aarhus: Universitetsforlaget I, 1960.

Hopkins, Dwight N., and Sheila Greeve Daveney (Editors). *Changing Conversations: Religious Reflection & Cultural Analysis.* New York: Routledge, 1996.

Horbury, William. *Messianism among Jews and Christians: Twelve Biblical and Historical Studies.* London: T. & T. Clark, 2003.

Hurh, Won Moo. *The Korean Americans.* Westport: Greenwood Press, 1998.

Hurh, Won Moo, and Kwang Chung Kim. *Korean Immigrants in America: A Structural Analysis of Ethnic Confinement and Adhesive Adaptation.* Rutherford: Associated University Presses, 1984.

Jacob, B. *Das erste Buch der Tora: Genesis übersetzt und erklärt.* Berlin: Schocken Books, 1934.

Kim, Byong-Suh, and Sang Hyun Lee (Editors). *The Korean Immigrant in America.* Montclair: The Association of Korean Christian Scholars in North America, Inc., 1980.

Kim, Heerak Christian. *Jewish Law and Identity: Academic Essays.* Cheltenham: The Hermit Kingdom Press, 2005.

Kim, Heerak Christian. *Toni Morrison's Beloved as African-American Scripture & Other Articles on History and Canon.* Cheltenham: The Hermit Kingdom Press, 2006.

Kim, Hyung-Chan (Editor). The Korean Diaspora: Historical and Sociological Studies of Korean Immigration and Assimilation in North America. Santa Barbara: ABC-Clio, Inc., 1977.

Kim, Warren Y. *Koreans in America.* Seoul: Po Chin Chai Printing Co. Ltd., 1971.

Koester, Helmut. *Introduction to the New Testament (Volume 1): History, Culture, and Religion of the Hellenistic Age.* New York: Walter de Gruyter & Co., 1982.

Kwak, Tae-Hwan, and Seong Hyong Lee (Editors). *The Korean-American Community: Present and Future.* Seoul: Kyungnam University Press, 1991.

Kwon, Ho-Youn, and Shin Kim (Editors). *The Emerging Generation of Korean-Americans.* Seoul: Kyung Hee University Press, 1993.

Lohfink, N. *Die Landverheissung als Eid: Eine Studie zu Gn 15.* Stuttgart: Katholisches Bibelwerk, 1967.

Major, Clarence. *The Dark and Feeling: Black American Writers and Their Work.* New York: The Third Press, 1974.

Mays, Benjamin E. *The Negro's God as Reflected in His Literature.* New York: Russell & Russell, 1938.

McEvenue, Sean E. *The Narrative Style of the Priestly Writer.* Rome: Biblical Institute Press, 1971.

Moberly, R. W. L. *Genesis 12-50.* Sheffield: JSOT Press, 1992.

Morey, Ann-Janine. "Toni Morrison and the Color of Life." *The Christian Century* 105 (November 16, 1988), pp. 1039-1042.

Morrison, Toni. "Behind the Making of *The Black Book.*" Black World 23 (February, 1974), pp. 86-90.

Morrison, Toni. *Beloved: A Novel.* New York: Vintage Books, 1987.

Morrison, Toni. "Rootedness: The Ancestor as Foundation" in *Black Women Writers (1950-1980): A Critical Evaluation.* Edited by Mari Evans. Garden City: Anchor Press/Doubleday, 1984.

Nitzan, Bilhah. *Qumran Prayer and Religious Poetry.* Translated by Jonathan Chapman. Leiden: E. J. Brill, 1994.

Petesch, Donald A. *A Spy in the Enemy's Country: The Emergence of Modern Black Literature.* Iowa City: University of Iowa Press, 1989.

Otten, Terry. *The Crime of Innocence in the Fiction of Toni Morrison.* Columbia: University of Missouri Press, 1989.

Park, Andrew Sung. *Racial Conflict and Healing: An Asian-American Theological Perspective.* Maryknoll: Orbis Books, 1996.

Rabin, C. "Alexaner Jannaeus and the Pharisees." *Journal of Jewish Studies* 7 (1956), pp. 3-11.

Rody, Caroline. *The Daughter's Return: African-American and Caribbean Women's Fictions of History.* New York: Oxford University Press, 2001.

Sailhamer, J. H. *The Pentateuch as Narrative: A Biblical-Theological Commentary.* Grand Rapids: Zondervan, 1992.

Sandmel, Samuel. *Philo of Alexandria: An Introduction.* New York: Oxford University Press, 1979.

Sarna, Nahum M. *Understanding Genesis.* New York: McGraw-Hill Book Company, 1966.

Schiffman, Lawrence. *The Eschatological Community of the Dead Sea Scrolls: A Study of the Rule of the Congregation.* Atlanta: Scholars Press, 1989.

Schneemelcher, Wilhelm (Editor). *New Testament Apocrypha.* Translated by Robert McLachlan Wilson. Louisvillle: Westminster/John Knox Press, 1991.

Schürer, Emil. *The History of the Jewish People in the Age of Jesus Christ (175 B.C.-A.D. 135): Volume II.* Revised and edited by Geza Vermes, Fergus Millar, and Matthew Black. Edinburgh: T. & T. Clark, 1979.

Schwartz, Daniel R. *Studies in the Jewish Background of Christianity.* Tübingen: J. C. B. Mohr (Paul Siebeck), 1992.

Solomon, Barbara H. (Editor). *Critical Essays on Toni Morrison's Beloved.* New York: G. K. Hall & Co., 1998.

162

Stone, Michael E. *Adam's Contract with Satan: The Legend of the Cheirograph of Adam*. Bloomington: Indiana University Press, 2002.

Stone, Michael E. *The Testament of Abraham: The Greek Recensions*. New York: Society of Biblical Literature, 1972.

Thomas, H. Nigel. *From Folklore to Fiction: A Study of Folk Heroes and Rituals in the Black American Novel*. New York: Greenwood Press, 1988.

Thompson, Thomas L. *Early History of the Israelite People: From the Written and Archaeological Sources*. Leiden: E. J. Brill, 1994.

Thompson, Thomas L. *The Historicity of the Patriarchal Narratives*. BZAW 133. Berlin: Walter De Gruyter, 1974.

Van Seters, J. *Abraham in History and Tradition*. New Haven: Yale University Press, 1975.

Wellhausen, J. *Die Komposition des Hexateuchs und der historischen Bücher des Alten Testaments*. Berlin: W. de Gruyter, 1963.

Wilkinson, Nicole. "'The Getting of Names': Anti-Intertextuality and the Unread Bible in Toni Morrison's *Song of Solomon* and *Beloved*." *Semeia*. No. 69/70 (1995), pp. 235-246.

Williamson, Paul R. *Abraham, Israel and the Nations: The Patriarchal Promise and its Covenantal Development in Genesis*. Sheffield: Sheffield Academic Press, 2000.

Wolfson, Harry Austryn. *Philo: Foundations of Religious Philosophy in Judaism, Christianity, and Islam*. Cambridge: Harvard University Press, 1947.

Yuh, Ji-Yeon. *Beyond the Shadow of Camptown: Korean Military Brides in America*. New York: New York University Press, 2002.

Index